KV-371-134

If you are unable to order this book from your local bookseller,
you may order directly form MusiVation International, LLC.
Quantity discounts are available.

Conversations
on
Money, Sex & Spirituality
with
Wilma and Michele

Edited by Michele Blood

For Information write:
Michele's MusiVation International, LLC
P.O. Box 12933
La Jolla, CA 92039
USA
or call : 800-547-5601
Fax : 858-459-3032
e-mail : MusiVation@aol.com
Web site : http://www.MusiVation.com

Dedication

We dedicate this book to our greatest teacher
and most precious gift from God, LIFE!
Thank You Life for all that you so freely,
lovingly and abundantly give.

"Two masters of conversation...Michele and Wilma have a style that flows as you learn. This book is fun to read and is an asset to any business that wants to be people focused. Pick it up, share it, and enjoy while you learn."
Raymond Justice, Entrepreneur, Executive coach and Author of "The Partner Up Method" and "Power of Intuition."

"Conversations with Wilma and Michele is an example of the depth of sharing possible between women friends; lets the reader meet two marvelous women who know and share their magnifence; it is so uplifting and useful and provides the reader with lovely affirmation/prayer pages to copy and frame."
Rev. Margo Ganster, Spiritual Coach and Seminar Leader.

"This wonderful book by Wilma and Michele is like listening in on two dear friends discussing vital areas of life in a refreshing, new and different way. These two womens' words are rich with wisdom and spiritual awareness. I especially like the gift at the end of each chapter. Find the ideas that "ring true" for you,...the ones which can transform your own life in so many areas. Begin now!"
Rev. Joy Almass, Personal Success Coach.

"A breath of fresh air for women! Sit down and enjoy a cup of tea with Wilma and Michele. Be refreshed and rejuvenated in the deepest part of your soul...feeling greatly encouraged to love, to live and create all good things! Men! Read only if you dare and only if you can handle more meaningful relationships with women!"
Karie Clingo, mother of five, and Author of "The Laughing Mother."

"It's just like being there in person - enjoying a cozy chat with two remarkable women - all about life's meaning and purpose and who you really are. The warmth, intimacy and powerful insights found in this book are treasures that will make a huge and positive difference in your life."
Valerie Cragin, Author of "The Road Manager" and "Photographic Modeling," Divisional Vice President(retired), Playboy Ent.

Wilma McIntyre
BIO

Wilma recognized her own Spirituality in the early 90's after going through major challenges in her life. In 1988, Wilma owned two well-known real estate franchise offices-just as the real estate market was on the downturn. At that time, she was trying to keep the offices going, but ended up losing all of her life savings and many accumulated properties; she kept hoping everything would turn around.

During this time, Wilma was covering up the pain with alcohol by drinking to excess at night! She was unhappy in her long-time marriage. Basically nothing was working, and Wilma was miserable. Wilma made the commitment to be alcohol-free. At this time, it seemed to Wilma that everything was tumbling down and crashing around her. In the midst of her crisis, Wilma started going to a series of workshops by Bob Proctor and other success coaches. That is where Wilma met Michele as Michele was hired to sing and lecture in the U.S.A. from Australia. Wilma, at that time, had released everything in her life-her possessions and her husband of 38 years, and started her life all over.

When Michele moved to the U.S.A., she reconnected with Wilma and introducing Wilma to deeper psychological and spiritual studies. From that point on, Wilma has unified so solidly with Success and Spirituality that she is now, after years of study, a success coach and spiritual counselor. Wilma is now dedicated to studying and teaching others how they can be successful, and change their lives for the positive.

Wilma now resides by the beach in La Jolla, California and is a very successful realtor in La Jolla where she enjoys a prosperous, joy-filled life.

MICHELE BLOOD

Michele electrifies every audience. She is a dynamic, world class act. Her recorded and written works have the power to literally change your life. She discovered MusiVation™ after a near fatal car accident and not only healed her body but she also went ahead and created great success in her life using her own MusiVation™ discovery.

Many of the world's greatest teachers use her material for their own personal benefit. Michele has worked with many of the worlds leading authorities in metaphysics teachers including **Deepak Chopra, Wayne Dyer, Jack Canfield, Tony Alessandra, Jim Cathcart, Bob Proctor** and many more. **Brian Tracy,** world authority on self-improvement says: *"Michele has put together materials that bring about permanent behavioral change. There is something in the human being that is naturally drawn by music, and you do not need to have any musical ability at all; all you have to do is hear the message combined with the music and it becomes part of you forever."*

Michele has been gifted with the awareness and the unprecedented talent to successfully impact people, intellectually, emotionally and physically. MusiVation™ is quickly becoming an industry in itself and has assisted hundreds of thousands of people and many companies all over the world to create well being and great success in every area of their life. Due to our growing market, MusiVation™ products and seminars have expanded into business, sales, relationships, health and weight control industries.

Michele Blood is a successful, multi-talented lady with a diverse business arena. In addition to Michele's MusiVation™ products and seminars, she also performs music concerts and sings at other venues worldwide.

An Introduction To
CONVERSATIONS WITH WILMA AND MICHELE

Hi! From Wilma and Michele...

This book is about how two friends helped each other grow spiritually through wonderful conversations. We both found that we had never before really connected with another friend in such an open, honest and spiritual level as we did together.

Each morning we would go to the beach, or to one another's home and do affirmative prayers and dialogue. We would examine our feelings and take them to such a high level that if either of us were depressed at the time, it certainly wasn't true after our conversations. They were uplifting and positive. During this time we had many challenges in our respective lives and were able to overcome them. After we had shared our feelings about what was going on and really discussed them, we would then do what we call "affirmative prayer". In this book, after each of the topics are discussed, we have a page with an affirmation-prayer for you to use every day in your life. These affirmations will assist you in changing your old thoughts to new and positive ideas and to assist you in creating the good you desire to come into your life. You will better understand what this actually means as you read the book. Even if any of it sounds ridiculous and impossible, please read on, as it will ring bells for you in some areas of your life, if not all. You would not even be reading this far unless you had decided that you desire to better understand how you can create more good in your life. And YOU CAN! These conversations cover topics about so many different areas, so that we can all grow and learn how to create abundance in all areas of our lives. That is why we call it, "Multi-Dimensional Abundance." For abundance is not just money, it also covers love, relationships, career, sex and much more. It is the experience of how to create more good in all areas of life.

Our conversations were so meaningful that after about 2 years we thought, "Wouldn't it be great to share this with others so they may benefit as we have!" That is where the idea of this book came about. We would take a subject and then have a passionate conversation, listening to each other's views and supporting each other, so as to grow in spiritual awareness. With each idea, our energy would get to a higher and higher level. We all have our challenges and problems. We can all overcome them, as there is always a solution....this you will read in our message to you. There is no challenge or problem that cannot be turned into a positive, or a gift. It is all in one's attitude and awareness of spiritual self. A friend once said to us, "I don't know how to get spiritual." We told him that each of us has the Spirit within us... we just have to open up to it.

Titling this book, "Conversations with Wilma and Michele," was our fun way of acknowledging the great book of Neal Donald Walsch, "Conversations with God". It is not however, anything like his wonderful book. It is simply two great friends discussing the many topics of life that we all have to face and work through. We simply thought it was a fun title. We know that having fun and finding joy in our lives is so very important. We do however, highly recommend Neal's books to everyone.

Our purpose is, that this book opens you more to the Spirit within and increases your awareness of your powerful, beautiful, spiritual Self. We had such a fun time writing this book! It started simply with the two of us in conversation. Our desire is that you will also enjoy and benefit by these pages as much as we have!

Much love and all good!
Wilma and Michele

(P.S. We feel that it is of utmost importance to surround ourselves with positive images and words, so please copy any of the affirmation prayer pages, to frame and hang up in your environment.)

TABLE OF CONTENTS

Definitions

(The following are definitions of some words that we use in our conversations) ☺

Metaphysical:
Above or beyond the physical.

Multi-Dimensional Abundance:
A flow of abundance in all areas of one's life including: joy, peace, sensuality, harmony, love, beauty, spiritual awareness, prosperity, health, peace and success.

Collective unconscious:
The collective consciousness of thoughts created by the whole human race. We are subject to many causes that lie within the collective mind and sometimes we can mistakenly think those thoughts are our own thoughts.

Treatment:
Affirmative prayer.

Affirmation:
An affirmation is a positive statement that is repeated over and over again to implant confidence-building thoughts into your subconscious mind. These new thoughts replace old negative ideas and beliefs into new and positive ones. They must be stated in the NOW, personalized and emotionalized. Eventually, the subconscious mind picks up these new thoughts and begins to draw to you, just like a magnet, all of the new thoughts you have implanted. The subconscious mind believes this is the truth right now as the subconscious mind is subjective and only knows NOW!

Practitioner:
A person who has been trained to professionally serve the spiritual growth of others through prayer, counseling and teaching.

Consciousness:
The outpicturing of what is in your mind through your thoughts. Everything you have thought, said, or have done. You can change your consciousness by changing your thinking.

Paradigm:
Our conditioned image. A compilation of ALL of our thoughts, words, actions, and habits.

Prosperity consciousness.
The outpicturing of what you believe prosperity means in your life.

Positivity:
A new, fun word for living a positive life, with a positive attitude.

Knowingness:
Another word to absolutely know that all is well. Faith!

Absadoodle: ☺
Absolutely:)

How to Achieve Multi-Dimensional Abundance in Your Life

Michele: Here we are in beautiful Ensenada! What a great setting for us to write this book Wilma and to continue our conversations about growing our awareness with Spirit.

Wilma: Ensenada! Yes, it is so beautiful. We are truly blessed and getting you away from it all was the only thing I could think of to finally have this idea of ours come to fruition. I know how important it is to take action on an idea when the guidance is so loud and clear. What a beautiful day it is to begin! The beautiful light patterns on the palm trees and on the rocks reflect God's light back to us. It makes me want to say, "Oh, Great Spirit, earth, sun, sky, and sea...you are inside and all around me!"

Michele: Wow! A miracle made you say it (laughing). I would also like to thank God right now for the words that are flowing through us in perfect harmony and love. I would also like to thank Karie Clingo, Scott768, Sandra Shahan, Sue Toftee and Jennifer Henry for their love and support with typing all of the conversation tapes. We love you friends! Let's start this conversation with one of my favorite topics...

Wilma: ...And that would be?

Michele: ATTITUDE girlfriend, Attitude! Attitude! Attitude!

"A positive attitude is useless unless it promotes positive action!"

Attitude

Wilma: Our attitudes are, the absolutely most important thing in life in order to change our lives to the positive, and as you have said here, Michele, it must also promote positive action. How we look at things and our paradigms. To have the willingness to shift our thoughts so that they are in perfect alignment with the Infinite is vital. It is so important to be able to pay attention to our thoughts, because our thoughts are the ones that give us our tomorrows. In life, whatever we think WILL come about and the attitude we have will create wonderful tomorrows. The challenge with this, Michele, is continuing to watch our thoughts because we're surrounded by what I call the "collective consciousness" or the "collective unconscious" where people seem to dwell on the negative. But really, if you look at it, there's so much more positive than negative going on in the world as long as we don't focus on the world news media too much. This promotes bad news. They think bad news sells and you know what? That is because it does! Bummer!

Michele: Absadoodle Wilma, we simply have to switch our attention, just like switching stations on the TV or radio.

Wilma: I mean, the media nearly always comes up with the negative stuff on the news, they don't say the positive stuff but, if you look at the world, it is 90% positive. Looking at all the good that's going on and focusing on the good continually, will bring more good back to you. I know that because I have seen it so much, and I also know that, as I become clearer, I begin to experience good in so many ways. Like you said Michele, I switch my station and focus on the good. In the beginning of retraining my thinking to switch to the positive, there were times that I had to keep shifting my thoughts. It might even have been a thousand times in one day because I was experiencing, after I had left my husband, so many negative thoughts.

Michele: Right, so what did you do?

Wilma: Well, I placed sticky notes all over my house that said, "Shift!" (chuckling)

Michele: Ah, I remember those!

Wilma: And then, I would immediately shift my present thought to the positive and take a deep breath, as it is so important to do this also and say, "SHIFT!"

Michele: Bob Proctor, our dear friend who wrote, "You Were Born Rich", says that it is a very powerful way to refocus by simply saying out loud "Shift!". I love that it is such a simple and yet immediate technique....

Wilma: It sure is! I would then state what I DO want to experience in my life. That I want love, happiness, peace of mind and joy. That's what I wanted then as well. So each time I would go into that depression, I would say "Shift!" (chuckling) After a while, I was crying and I was screaming it out! I was doing all kinds of things, but it took that to shift my thinking and I was so ready to feel good again. My will is now stronger, so it is much easier because I went through that powerful exercise and I'm so grateful for it. To know that now I catch myself thinking good thoughts. Jesus said that, "When you judge, judge right." Judge for the positive. You could catch yourself in a negative judgement on someone so easily, but take that and shift it to judging right. You can live your life with this continually and uppermost in your mind. Phenomenal things will happen that bring so much good to you and you too, will be forever grateful when new positive experiences become the norm.

Michele: Yes! That's great because all our attitude is, as psychology study has taught us, is the sum total today of everything that has gone before, not only of our direct ancestry but also from inherited tendencies from their ancestry. We are more or less the entire experience of the human race since the first face turned from the cloud. We are, in a way, the result of what happened yesterday. Therefore, that is where we get the accumulation of the sum total of all that's gone before, including in others' lives. That's why we really can start beginning to change our attitude by changing our nows, which will then change our entire future to one of positivity. It's just habit. Our attitude is an accumulation of all of our past habits. So, if someone says, "You've got a bad attitude," it's because the accumulation of all your past thoughts and actions and thinking process has been in a negative vibration. This does not make you a bad person, as that is the past. However, now we can all consciously choose to create good thoughts and then everyone will be commenting on your great attitude. When people say to me, "Oh Michele people cannot change", I simply say, "Rubbish....SHIFT!!!" (laughs) So yes, what you were doing with all of your sticky notes Wilma, is causing a new habit, a new habit of thinking, which then changed your attitude to a positive attitude. That is so great that you were disciplined enough to do this a thousand times a day saying, "Shift!," like Bob Proctor suggests, or saying, "Next!", an idea from Mark Victor Hanson the author of, "Chicken Soup For The Soul". It's such a great way to just simply shift thought because it's an everyday discipline and because the attitudes or the thoughts, like you said, are the collective unconscious of everybody on the planet. There are so many different negative thoughts out there that we could assimilate every day, hence it's an everyday discipline to surround ourselves with like-minded people that have a good, positive attitude.

Wilma: That is so true! To be with like-minded people, to keep that shifting going....

Michele: ...POSITIVE like-minded people....

Wilma: Yes! Excuse me (laughing)... POSITIVE, like-minded people. That's really interesting. Now that I'm so much stronger in my thinking, people that aren't that way when they come into my presence begin to think that way also; or, they simply leave (laughing). By my setting the example, if each of us can shift our thoughts and stay with the positive-i.e. setting the example for each person with whom we are in contact, then each person will be shifting for the next person and so on and so forth. It's so wonderful to see that expanding around you and to attract all these beautiful people. To attract good because you do have those right thoughts and the right thinking.

Michele: I know in the beginning, it is so important when we first make a decision, to have that absolute multi-dimensional abundance in our life. It really is important. Stop reading newspapers that have negativity. Don't watch all that negative television because our minds are visual. We think in pictures, so what we look at is extremely potent to the subconscious mind. The subconscious mind is totally subjective and takes it all in, thinking it's happening right now, and that is not going to help your attitude if you're watching negativity. There are tons of great things to watch on television of course, like my TV show, (laughing) "M-Power"...and there are tons of great people to be with. And you know sweetie, a friend of mine was concerned when he first got into this type of thinking because he said, "Oh, my parents are negative and blah, blah, blah....How can I be with my parents when all they look at is the bad in me?"....So I said, "Well, that's just reflecting back to you how you feel about yourself." Now only a year later he said, "Gosh, I loved it last time I was with my family! They're really nice to me." You see, when we change, it seems like the whole world has to! However, it is us that has changed and then how we think of ourselves is reflected back to us. Well, my friend really got it saying, "I see, because my attitude has changed, so everything around me seems to have also changed- including my parents...WOW!" Good on you mate!!

Wilma: Going back to TV. A lot of people watch the news before they go to bed and that's the absolute worst time to watch the news if you want to catch up. When I go to bed, I'll...

Michele: What do you mean, catch up?

Wilma: To catch up on the news, to find out what's going on. Some people just need, have to know...

Michele: You could find out what's going on without watching the news...

Wilma: ...Yes! However, the best way I use to go to sleep is to just think of all the things I'm grateful for and start thanking God for all the beauty. Think of every little thing. Sometimes you might have a challenge finding things to be grateful for. Just start right where you are if you're laying in bed and say, "Thank you, God, for the bed I'm in."

Michele: Oh yes...I do love my good, comfortable bed.

Wilma: Well, just keep going from there. Give thanks for everything that you have and then pretty soon, it just expands and expands and expands.

Michele: So, Attitude, Attitude, Attitude. Everybody can shift their thinking. However, I think it's important to never say to somebody if you think they're being negative, "Oh you're being so negative." We must remember that we all have old fears and old patterns. You will simply alienate your friends if you start correcting them. You be the example. The best person that you could help with changing your attitude is with yourself. Starting with myself, that's the only person I can help today with a positive attitude. If we are really upset and want to get out of a negative thought we have about someone, a great suggestion by Napoleon Hill, the author of "Think and Grow Rich," is to write it down in the sand on the seashore where no one can see it, and then simply let the sea and waves wash it away forever. Let it go! Wilma, by the way, your attitude is sparkling! It's wonderful and...

Wilma: ...And of course! (laughing)

Michele: And it's for real. That's Attitude.

Wilma: I was just thinking as I went for my little walk-we are talking about so many things that make up our experience to be in a multi-dimensional experience of abundance. Just being here with you Michele is such a gift! I mean, look at the gift of this beautiful place; the food, the beauty, the peacefulness and the joy. The absolute joy of just putting this together and the harmony, the flow of it all. This experience truly is multi-dimensional abundance.

Michele: Oh, peace, what a wonderful word, just the word fills me with peace. Mmmmmmmm...

Wilma: Being at peace and knowing that all is well, all of the time, is a discipline at first but, wow! Such an incredible experience. And I've seen so many things fall into place when at first things appeared to be in chaos in my life. By just staying in the knowing that all is well and the underlying is perfect, in perfect order. Yes, what a great affirmation, "All is well." Sometimes it takes the chaos, the breaking apart and then reassembling in order to see that it's all in perfect order. I have experienced that so many times, and then this summer was the perfect example when I was on that canoe trip. I had been canoeing in the wilderness for a week down the Missouri river. One morning I was awakened to; "Wilma, your canoe is missing." Apparently, the river rose during the night and the canoe floated down river. I kept my cool and knew that somehow all would work out-even though we were miles from anywhere-basically, up the river without a canoe. There was an extraordinary turn of events where someone had to go home because of a death in the family so I had a new canoe partner and everyone was taken care of. This enabled me to continue on with the trip. Later that day we found the canoe with all the missing gear in it and nothing was lost. All the time, I stayed at peace, knowing that all was well.

Michele: That is such a great demonstration Wilma! When we let go and we are not in fear, we can then have peace of mind. You achieved peace of mind when you were in the canoe situation because you knew that it would all be okay. That is faith! That is ATTITUDE with a capital A! Let us now affirm the truth!

Attitude

Today, right now, I am aware of the limitless possibilities in my life.

I choose to let go of the past and live in the now, knowing that everything I can possibly be is right here as part of my consciousness.

My attitude is positive and I always find solutions and see the good in all so called "challenges".
I look to no one for my good but recognize that everyone is a golden link in the chain of my good, as I am to them, when I think Right. I now think Right and see all the possibilities for good in my life. My thoughts are powerful and I know that these thoughts bring more and more good into my life.

I am happy now and I give thanks for the ability to be able to choose my thoughts.

I choose to be happy, free, likeable and prosperous.
I love my life and I live it to the fullest.

Thank you life for my happy and wonderfully positive ATTITUDE!

Notes

Attitude

1. Write a paragraph as to why a positive attitude is important.

2. Make a list of the areas you think an attitude change would be important to you.

3. Why is it important to pay attention to your thoughts?

4. Name a way you can change your thinking from negative to positive.

5. Why is what happened yesterday not important any longer?

6. How can you form a new positive habit?

7. Why is it important to stay away from negative thinking and other people's negative thinking?

8. What is important to do before you go to sleep?

9. Name some ways you can set a positive example.

10. Why are affirmations important?

11. Read aloud the affirmation on attitude 10 times today.

" To release the past
we must be able to
forgive "

–Anonymous

Forgiveness

Michele: Forgiveness is a word that is perhaps not always used with true meaning because when we truly forgive, we release the past for our own good and unblock those psychological, deep, hurt feelings that have been stopping our growth. You know, Wilma, how some people sort of say, "Well, I can't forgive them for what they have done," but it's for yourself that you're forgiving. Or people may say, "I can forgive but I can't forget what you have done." I feel that when we forgive with all of our heart, we do forget, as we do not hold onto the past any longer. We then take whatever has been and release it; only then are we released, and this includes forgiving ourselves. Edith R. Stauffer, from her book, "Unconditional Love and Forgiveness," has a lovely little poem. What is it Wilma?

Wilma: She has a little poem in here: "Forgiving ourselves... Some pray for things they have done and make them seem like double. Some straight away forgive themselves and save the Lord the trouble."

Michele: Oh, I love that!!!!!!

Wilma: But the forgiveness is so important as is the fact that you don't even ever have to go to that person to say, "I forgive you." I think that really prevents more people from forgiving, perhaps thinking that we have to forgive that person to their face. The thing is that we can forgive them in our own mind and then release them to their highest good. There are many ways of doing that, and once we get rid of that stuff in us that has been holding us back, perhaps because we are angry at this person or because we may have expected them to behave a certain way and they didn't behave that way.... Once we get rid of that, it leaves us so free, free to enjoy the beauty of life and the peace and harmony around us. We may have been literally blinded to all the good by our anger and pain. So the pain just kept popping up in unexpected situations with totally different people.

Michele: Oh yes, I remember forgiving one of my ex-boyfriends and how it was really painful because I felt like he had done so much harm to me emotionally. I said to myself that, he was this, and he was that, however, something deep within me realized that I was simply reflecting back to myself my own inner doubts and fears and that I had attracted him into my life to learn, forgive and then grow. He was, in fact, a gift in my life. To rise above and to know what I didn't want to experience next time, that's for sure. And you know what I went through with that one don't you, Wilma my dearest girlfriend? (laughing) Anyway, now that I've forgiven...you know what I did? I found the most powerful healing method...I wrote him a letter, and I just let it all out. I just wrote this letter and put down all the things that I felt angry about like, "You blah, blah, blah, question mark, you did this, blah, blah, blah; or, you weren't there for me ..... and what I really wanted was for you to be a man, a friend who could be loving, supportive and able to communicate and you weren't." I went on and on, and eventually, I really got it out and didn't feel as angry. I was on about my fifth page and all of a sudden I felt like I could forgive him. So, I wrote and said out loud, "However, I forgive you and I release you to your highest Divine good." I have always found it beneficial to attribute everything that is not for my highest Divine good to another's highest Divine good. I signed the letter and I really meant it when I signed, "Love, Michele." Then, I burned it. This is a powerful way to release hurt from our minds. But...I guess not everyone can burn a letter right where they are, in case the fire bells go off (laughs), but one can always rip it up. Rip it up into tiny, tiny pieces until you feel better. It is such a psychological release and boy, did it feel good! Now, I do this anytime something comes up when I need to release and forgive- be it a situation or relationship. What do you do Wilma? Give us your words of wisdom because I can only grow through learning more and more.

Wilma: Well, sometimes I'll write it and burn it or tear it up, but there's another process that I've been through that has been so effective for me. That is to have somebody real close to me or even a neutral party to facilitate, so that a lot of pent up emotions and hate and anger and who-knows-what-else with my ex-husband, could be released. I had been married for thirty-eight years and I didn't even know I was surrounded by all of that pain. I was just kind of like a little frog in a pot of water with the water temperature slowly heating and the frog staying in the hot water because the frog doesn't notice how dangerously hot the water has become and the poor little frog ends up on the menu of a French restaurant.

Michele: (laughing) You tell me my analogies are different ! I can't imagine ...knowing you now, that you have ever been miserable. You are such a happy person. Boy, that really did work for you Missy Frog!!!

Wilma: It sure did! I even went through this process of where a facilitator and I were together... And I was able to totally vent out everything I thought he did to me and how he hurt me; I was just yelling and screaming and pounding and doing all kinds of things unlike me. And then, I placed a chair in front of me and pretended it was him.

Michele: Well, that's good if you don't have someone that you could do the venting with, if you're just on your own....

Wilma: Yes, I did both. However, what I did was place this chair in front of me and I put something on the chair that reminded me of my ex....

Michele: (laughing) What was it.... (both laughing)?

Wilma: I don't even remember what it was because I was just so into visualizing him. I'm such a visual person.

Michele: You could just put a photograph there.

Wilma: Yes, if you are not a visual person that would work. Then the next step was, after I had vented and felt that I had let it all out,

I told him what I expected of him because when things go south like that, it's because of our expectations. It's not because of what the other person did. I said, "Well, I expected you to be this way and I expected you to be that way," you know. And then, after I got through all that, I released him from every single one of those expectations. I went all the way through every single one and then released him to his highest good and me to my highest good. After that, I just sat there meditating, feeling the light of God flowing through me and healing me. I had just totally released it. That has really kept me clear and that's one of the reasons why I am so happy and fulfilled today. I have compassion for myself.

Michele: I think it's a vital process to learn how to release and then forgive and also to remember as I said, to forgive ourselves. I mean, there are so many occasions I thought negative rubbish and there's so many things for which I wanted to forgive myself, and I feel so much better now. I release the past daily and learn what to do and how to respond, instead of reacting. Now, let us affirm that we always, in all right Divine ways, Forgive!

Forgiveness

I live to love and always forgive
I only speak the truth that I live
I forgive

Right now I forgive myself from any hurts
from the past.
I release hurt from my life.

I release everyone and everything
that is not for my highest good
to their highest good.
I go ahead this day with love
and I feel so wonderful
Because I forgive!

Notes

Forgiveness

1. Write at least a paragraph as to why it is important to forgive.

2. Write a letter to someone you thought hurt you. Express all the pain you felt..if you have to stop to cry or beat on a pillow or scream..Do it. Express all the feelings and get it out. Next write in the same letter what you expected of that person..how you expected them to treat you..etc. then one by one cancel out each expectation. Burn the letter or rip it up then release that person to his or her highest good. And you to your highest good. Then sit quietly and feel the light of God above you flowing through you, until you are totally immersed in the Divine light. Meditate in this light until you feel complete and at peace.
(Remember to breath! ☺)

3. As time goes on, you may need to write this forgiveness letter again. Call it a tune up. Clear out any remaining feelings and resentful, negative thoughts that may sometimes creep back into your consciousness.

4. Do this process for each person with whom you have a negative charge. Do not group people together, but rather, consider each person, one by one, over time, until you feel complete and at peace.

5. Repeat the forgiveness affirmation after each letter is completed.

"If you think of the universe as a vast electrical sea in which you are immersed and from which you are formed, opening to your creativity changes you from something bobbing in the sea to a more fully functioning, more conscious, more cooperative part of that ecosystem."

–Julia Cameron

Creativity

Wilma: Every one of us has creativity within us and many of us don't even recognize it. I didn't recognize that I was creative at all, until people started telling me and utilizing my creativity. You know, a lot of people don't recognize the creativity within them. When things come really easy for an individual, and others pay you compliments on this ease, you may find yourself just discounting it, e.g. "Oh no, that was nothing." But that's the beauty of it; that's where our gifts are-in our creative power. I've seen it time and time again with people who write. My daughter writes beautiful poetry, and yet, she doesn't want to put it out there 'cause it was "nothing" to her, you know.

Michele: Well, I guess she just enjoys it now, simply for the pleasure of writing. It doesn't really matter as long as it gives us personal fulfillment. If it is not, then that is a different story. Whatever gives us fulfillment when we're creating something, it doesn't necessarily mean that we have to have other people admire it or give it accolades. It's just fulfillment of what we're doing. You know, Wilma, so many people enjoy painting; however, if they went to an art critic and received a negative opinion... well, that could destroy their motivation to paint freely, diminish their intrinsic enjoyment of their art and halt their creative expression which once flowed unencumbered. Of course, I am referring to those people who truly do it as a hobby and not solely for the income. Getting back to this wonderful topic, I feel that when we are in touch with our unity with Spirit, creativity is as natural as breathing. That, to me, is what it's all about. For when we are affirming and knowing what it is in our lives that we're at one with, we feel creative and all is in the flow. Sometimes people say that they've got writer's block....Well, I know if I ever feel like that with my song writing or whatever, I just know that I need to be silent, be still and unify myself with spirit. Then the creativity that's universal begins to flow. It was always present. I simply had to be still and feel it.

Wilma: Yes, the flow is a good thing. In the past, if I wanted to give a talk, I used to write everything out and then stick to that form. But then, I would forget it when I would be in front of people, and I would be trying to think of my talk...with all those people looking at me. I would forget everything. (laughs) But now, I just start with a general idea and ask God for the words, that will have the most impact for them, or maybe some thoughts they could take with them that day so that it will be life changing. This way my words flow. It's just so neat when you just kinda open up and let the creative spirit of God flow through you and give you the words and they just come out and you say, "Did I say that?" (laughs)

Michele: You know, I love that book Wilma, "The Artist's Way," by Julia Cameron. She speaks about writing every single day in a personal journal. Some people call this journaling. You know, I don't exactly journal. What I do to pray in the mornings is to write it all down. However, as Julia says in her wonderful book, "It really doesn't matter what you write as long as you write" and boy do I love to write my prayer treatments! Committing the truth to paper is a very powerful exercise. I love that book because it's really good discipline for people to learn to just write whatever is coming out of your thought process and to see what has been hiding in there ready to be planted or released. The more you write, the more your creativity flows. It doesn't matter whether you're an accountant, a baker, a policeman, or whatever it is that you do, because creativity gives you your passion and joy back. It has always been there waiting for us to WAKE UP! Speaking of bakers, pass me a piece of toast, will you sweetie?

Wilma: (laughs) Julia Cameron, in her book, has where you write what she calls, "Morning pages." It consists of getting up in the morning and simply writing anything that pops into your head.

Michele: Yes, that's it exactly. You know what I love? I love to watch children be creative and you know what else?

Wilma: (laughing) What?

Michele: I think we can all be more creative when we don't worry about what other people think because then, we are doing our own thing. Little kids aren't thinking about if it will look funny if they hop, skip and jump.

Wilma: That is so true, Michele. By removing all the barriers around us and not caring about what other people think is another important key to creativity.

Michele: It is great to create something UNIQUE! Nothing new would ever be invented if it weren't for those creative souls who didn't "give a hoot" about what other people said.

Wilma: Oh yes, now let's eat! This restaurant is so pretty on the ocean.

Michele: Speaking of pretty, that guy over at that table sure is.... So Wilma, now that we are on the topic of not worrying about what other people think, if I would say something totally sensual to that guy sitting over there and if anyone else heard me, would you be embarrassed? Come on, truly Wilma..... (laughing)!

Wilma: Na, I'd just laugh.

Michele: Well, he is very cute. However, let's keep chatting instead. I LOVE our conversations. However... I must acknowledge that God was being very creative when he molded that fine human vessel! (Both laugh) Thinking about creativity Wilma, I also feel that when I am joyous and having fun, I am more in my creative flow. So, when I am not feeling creative, I know I need to stop taking it all so seriously and have some fun!

Wilma: Me too. I have to wait until it flows again.

Michele: What you just said is really true....Sometimes you just have to wait until it flows. So just unify with Spirit and keep affirming; "I absolutely know that I am creative and that creativity flows through me NOW." Then go and have some fun with whatever fun means to you...like a good old-fashioned bubble bath, a walk in nature, roller-blading...anything that is fun to you!

Wilma: (laughs) As you say Michele, absadoodle! When I am in a creative mode, I like to look out at nature and only then do I feel One with it all and allow it to flow through me.

Michele: Oh that is so beautiful Wilma, you woman of nature! On that note, let's go into prayer right now.

Creativity

I am one with all the good there is in life. All that I think is creative new thoughts. I love my life and I let all that the Divine Mind has and is, flow through me into all of my creative pursuits. I love all that I do and all that I do is in harmony and love. Right now I am in the creative flow of the Divine. I give thanks for this flow of creativity in all areas of my beautiful and fulfilling life. I am the creative flow of life now.

And So it Is

Notes

Creativity

1. Name several things you do that is very easy for you.

2. Name your deepest desires.

3. Why is it important for you to express your gifts to others?

4. Why is it good to journal every day?

5. Start a journal and write in it every morning...at least 3 pages. Write what comes to mind. It doesn't have to make sense...just anything. The important thing is just to write!

"That which we make ourselves
mentally, we become unified
with physically.
If your thought always relates
you to disease,
then your thought becomes
a fixed power
to cause disease within you:
and if your thought always relates
you to health,
then your thought becomes a fixed
power exerted to keep you well."

-Wallace Wattles

Health and Healing

Michele: I love that quote from Mr. Wattles! That is the truth. However, it can become confusing when we first start thinking healing thoughts and still feel sick. For example somebody told me just the other day that she was affirming that her sinuses are clear and healthy, but then she said, " But then, I feel guilty like I am not doing the right thing because I still feel sick. I still feel like my sinuses are full," And I said, "Yes, that's from the cause, the cause of the original thought, and it also comes from the collective unconscious as well as our own thoughts, so that there is nothing about which to feel guilty." I told her that she can effect change by changing the cause, which then, in turn, changes the effect. The health and clear-breathing bit she still didn't quite get. But then, she must have, to some degree, because she began to feel better. You are not in denial of what you're experiencing, but instead, you're real-izing that the truth is that you are perfect, whole and complete. You can actually change the cause and have the effect be perfect health. We must always acknowledge our fears and our pain. That is our wake up call to find out and release what is really going on at a deeper level. Perhaps forgiving someone from our past is required for the healing of our bodies (see Forgiveness chapter). We must never blame ourselves or feel guilty because we are in pain or feel-ing sick. We are here, after all, experiencing a physical event, and therefore, it is natural to feel all things-the so-called "good" and "bad" of the physical world. Where there is an up, there must be a down. Denying this will not change gravity. If we jump out of a window, then we will fall...as long as you're not good mates with a guy called "Superman" who has been flying around the neighbor-hood (laughs).

Wilma: Although, you know Michele, a lot of people have trouble really understanding that. I ran into a gal the other day, a friend I have known for many years who said she's experiencing a toxic syndrome. She was allergic to her workplace, and she was just feeling awful and had to quit working. She kept claiming how awful she felt. So, I just started her off with an affirmation that each time she felt that way to say, "I am a radiant, vibrant, dynamic, healthy woman." She looked at me and said, "I'm feeling so terrible, how can that help?" I replied, "That's the best moment to be saying it and affirming it. When you feel really bad, remember to just keep affirming that you are one with all that is, and that you are in perfect, radiant health. Affirm it over and over and over again." Well, at least this helped her to get started in a positive direction even though it may have seemed crazy to her at the time. She had nothing to lose,except ill health!

Michele: Wilma, remind me when we get back home, to give her my "Create Miracles" tape. It is such a good tape for affirming good health and a positive attitude. As you know, these positive songs with the positive lyrics assisted in my own healing of my own body, after my car accident. Yes, I am plugging my MusiVation™ tapes. However, that is why I created them...to assist others in waking up to the truth; plus I love the music! Hearing the music with the words is really wonderful because the words go straight into your subconscious mind. So, when you really can't say, "I feel good", then put on the music. James Brown, how I love ya! I feel that his lyrics are such a powerful affirmation, "I feel good and I knew that I would." Wow, now that is powerful!

Wilma: I am not that acquainted with Mr. Brown, as we are from a different era. However, it sounds good to me!

Michele: Well trust me, he is awesome. Do you know what else is also wonderful, besides our beloved Mr. Brown, the King of Soul? It is REALLY knowing that you are attracting like-minded friends and beautiful people so that they can know the truth for you. Wilma, you have always kicked me in the butt when I was feeling down. You have never let me wallow or allowed me to stay stuck in that yucky, negative stuff. You've known the truth for me, and I thank God for our friendship every single day! I think that you are such a gift to this woman-to know the truth! To know the truth for another is affirming the truth for ourselves. Just being here and talking about this great stuff and knowing that it will be in a book is so amazing, and we are having so much fun doing it! This is the truth for the healing of life and this can be the truth for everybody....

Wilma: It is just so beautiful to know that we can take responsibility and take control of our lives. Knowing that we have the power to allow spirit to flow through us, through our very own thinking...with our words and our feelings, and also as you said, Michele, the music. Just putting those affirmations to music is so powerful-even if somebody makes up a little tune that works for them and then sings the affirmations.....

Michele: Whistle while you work.!

Wilma: Yes! (whistling and both laughing) Having done that in the past, I remember that the demonstration was so powerful and almost immediate; I'd say within 24 hours... I made it into a melody for the woman about whom I just told you. I encouraged her to make a tune of, "I am radiant, vibrant, dynamic and healthy," and to sing it with some kind of music that she likes. Then, I'm certain she'll remember to go over and over and over her affirmations again. Yes, this is just like your powerful, affirmation pop songs. They change one's thoughts so very quickly. The melody and lyrics are just there for good!

Michele: Yes, for our good (smiling)! I remember hearing our friend Jackie say, "Oh Gosh, the flu is going around. Yeah, it's going around all right; right AROUND me and out the door" (laughing). I loved that because it's just a thought you know. Somebody said, "Well, it's the winter so I always get a cold," and I replied, "So move to a place where it's the summer and then you won't catch anything."

Wilma: Yes, everyone comes here to Mexico to sit in the sun and have some FUN!

Michele: Now lets all affirm our perfect health.

I AM HEALED!

I absolutely know that I live in an abundantly healthy, wonderful universe. My world is filled with health and vitality. I know that this is the truth and I absolutely focus on the health and on the good because I live in the One Mind and act through the One Body, in accord with Divine harmony, perfection, and poise. Every organ of my body moves in absolute accord with perfect harmony. Divine intelligence circulates through me automatically, spontaneously and perfectly. Every single cell of my being is directed and animated by Divine perfection and Divine harmony. I absolutely know that every cell of my being is smiling and happy and healthy. I now release every single cell that isn't happy. I release it. It is gone, knowing that as the little cells are holding hands, they are all becoming happy, healthy, wonderful cells, and that there is healing and glowing health in every area of my life.

As I cast out any memories and any thoughts that have thought otherwise and only see the growth and health and the light of love, the healing light all through my entire body. The healing light is in my body right now, flowing through every cell and between the cells. The perfect healing light is in this continuous flow every moment of my being. Because I am healed, I know I am. I love myself. I am my best friend.

And so it is

Notes

Health and Healing

1. Why is it important to keep your thoughts on health instead of disease?

2. What is the benefit of pain and illness?

3. Why are musical affirmations more effective?

4. Why is it important for you to take responsibility for your life and how you feel?

" Sex energy is the creative
energy of all geniuses.
There never has been, and
never will be a great
leader, builder, or artist
lacking in this driving
force of sex. "
–Napoleon Hill

SEX

Wilma: Sex, wow! A topic of many different connotations and conversations. However, we don't really talk about it much Michele, so I am looking forward to this conversation. You know, since I've been totally involved in my spiritual practice, I've rediscovered sex and found that sex is now a totally spiritual experience. To be unified with God and unified with my partner at the same time,to be totally and completely present for my partner; it has been such a joyous experience for me, an experience that I had never encountered before in my life.

Michele: Yes, Unification not fornication! (laughing) Well, I think if you're talking about sex, then sex is creative energy. To me, it is the creative energy which IS God, and God sure knows how to create great experiences for us (laughing)! The Infinite does not make mistakes. The sexual energy to procreate is the most powerful energy on the physical plane. It's the life force, the driving energy behind everything. I think it's really important to understand and become educated about this powerful energy so that we can use it for good in our lives. To learn how to do this, read Napoleon Hill's chapter on sexual energy in his book, "Think and Grow Rich." He said that the most successful people he has studied were highly sexual. However, that does not mean that these people had sex all the time. He said that they simply re-channeled that creative energy into creative pursuits, such as their work. They found something about which to be passionate. When we are in our creative mode, we then become passionate about living life, and that passion can be called sexual energy. I feel that, when we have fulfilling experiences, that IS sexual energy. It's not necessarily about "having sex."

Wilma: I totally agree. However, that puts a whole new light on sex!

Michele: Yes, thank goodness! When one is experiencing sex with one's partner, it's great and it's free; but as you said Wilma, when you are truly aligned as a whole person who is really feeling your own unity with God and then you find another person who is also truly aligned as a whole person...well, then the experience becomes pure magic that goes way beyond the actual sex act itself. Sex is unification of spirit. So many people have too many sexual hang-ups; sex can be one of the most freeing experiences on earth when we love who we are and just allow our selves to let go and be in the moment. A lot of the old paradigms about sex are still so prevalent in today's society, and this really needs to be released from how we feel about a truly beautiful experience.

Wilma: The passion and the creative energy is so beautiful. When we have passion in our life, we can really experience life to it's full-ness. We can experience everything, embracing every moment of our lives, and having the knowing-ness that whatever we do is the right, perfect thing to do. I like to do a lot of outdoor stuff, like canoeing and cycling, but I have also started doing a lot more creative things now that the passion in my life has ignited. That is sexual energy. I can really express myself now. There is so much fun in being able to express our feelings and who we are. I love seeing the beautiful in everything now, including sex. I now see the beautiful creativity all around me and live in that passion. That is LIFE! Yes! Yes! Yes!

Michele: Wilma, it is so great to hear you talk about sex like this! I am so happy for you because I know you had been through so much pain in your past. When I was with a partner for a while, and it was based on sex and sex alone, I didn't even realize it at the time. I know we had real sexual chemistry, but we didn't have anything else going. It was really unfulfilling, and it became very damaging and affected negatively every area in my life,including my business. I was just so caught up in him that it took me a while to see the light and move on.

Wilma: I think I know who you are talking about (laughs). But you know Michele, don't be so hard on yourself. You bounced right back as soon as it was over. It is sometimes so difficult for us to see it when we are in the midst of experiencing it. Sexual experiences are so beautiful with like-minded people. That is why it is so good to be friends first.

Michele: You are so right, sweetie! Now that I have chosen to abstain from sex for a while, I feel so empowered and wonderful about who I am now. I will always wait until it truly feels right and that I really like the person. It's been quite a while, mmmm....

Wilma: A long time! Well, ten months to you may be a long time (laughing)! It's all relative. My abstinence was literally years, and I was even married at the time!

Michele: I guess it's how you define "a long time (also laughing)!" This time is allowing me to have that passion of life, to feel like a whole person again... and it's GREAT! It's a wonderful feeling to know, that next time, it will be very different, as I will have learned from my past. Of course, I have also had wonderful, very fulfilling happy sexual experiences in the past. However, it is truly amazing how one unhappy experience can teach us. Well, I'll put it this way, now, I know what I don't wish to experience! I love Wendy Keller's new book, "The Cult Of The Born Again Virgin." This book, even though it is written for women, is a book that I believe from which anyone can grow and learn how chosen celibacy is a great thing. I don't feel that refraining from sex simply because we cannot find a partner is truly a good experience in itself or even considered "true celibacy" because we are still in the process of sizing up potential sexual partners. Wendy writes in her very powerful book about choosing to be celibate for a while to heal and unify with our spirit so that it is a totally empowering feeling and great for one's self-esteem. Have you read it yet Wilma?

Wilma: Yes, I have, and I absolutely loved it. A must read!

Michele: I really feel good about myself now and have my own confidence and energy back. I feel an ecstasy now that I had not experienced for quite a while, just simply breathing in life. Ecstasy is that feeling when I am really feeling my oneness with God. I get "heart glow" to the max! I guess, these days, so many people are focusing on and are concerned about catching diseases that (and I totally agree with safe sex for many reasons) I have become very aware of my potential partner's awareness of this issue too. One's attitude and thought processes... this to me is the most important thing. Wow....I mean, Wilma, since I would never have someone in my business who had a negative attitude, I certainly would make sure that the person with whom I share my body is definitely in a good positive vibration! (Wilma laughing now) No, really Wilma, I am serious, because you are totally immersed in that person. It is not only bodily fluids you are exchanging, but also each other's energy and aura. You can actually take on their energy, and so it's important to know what a person THINKS.

Wilma: Honey, I am not laughing at you. It's just unusual to see you so serious. Go girl! Tell it like it is!

Michele: (Smiling) I guess I am pretty "gung ho" about this topic. Yes, passion! I love what Stuart Wilde says in his book, "Life Wasn't Meant To Be A Struggle:" when you meet and straight away have sex, then it can be very challenging to remain in your individuality and to really get to know the person.

Wilma: Why?

Michele: Well, first of all, he says that if you begin a relationship where it is NOT sexual straight off, then you have more time to really get to know each other on a different level. You will probably find out things about your partner about which you may have never found out, if you had had sex straight away. If you are in a relationship that started off straight under the sheets, Mr. Wilde informs us that it is a very healthy thing to have times where we abstain from sex, to get reacquainted-where both of you can have times where you can really get connected to each other's spirit.... like when you were a teenager and dating was such fun! You probably remember having a great experience simply holding hands! It is wonderful to remember the handholding, the little glances and all that stuff that makes it all so magical and sweet-oh, and the cuddling; I could really get back into that. I know that men need cuddling just as much as us women, even if they won't admit it! However, my dear friend, I am rolling on now. Tell me how it was for you after you first became a single woman subsequent to all those years of marriage.

Wilma: Hmmm, let me see... MUCH BETTER!!!!!!! Now I feel free to be me. However, that is only because I was in an unhappy marriage for so long. Lots of people are blessed and can learn to grow and learn together and I do pray that I will also find that in my life with a partner. I also know that I must feel fully whole and not ever again be just another "half." I now enjoy the passion of who I am. I had to totally get away from the negative energy and take a couple of years to figure out who I really was before I even started dating. I mean, I didn't know. I was so involved in somebody else's energy for 38 years..... yes that's how long it was. It was a LONG TIME. And then, as soon as I was starting to figure out who I was, I could expand. I guess we can talk more about relationships in another chat. However, let's face it, if you are engaged in sex, then you are in a relationship....even if it is only physical. We do, however, pray that we can all wake up to how shallow and unfulfilling these types of so called "quickies" can be (laughs).

Michele: Your getting pretty hip there, Wilma!

Wilma: (still laughing) Hanging out with you can do some pretty weird and magical things my friend! However, we must know that the relationship we have with ourselves must come first so that we can be a great and supportive, healthy two WHOLES! (laughing)

Michele: So well put my dear! Keep going, I am loving this.

Wilma: It's true, because your partner is a reflection of yourself or your fears that come up. We know that things can get very emotional in our relationships as they do bring out who we really are deep down inside, and we can learn so much in a relationship about what we need to heal. That is why it is so important to be very choosy about with whom we begin and take time to get to know them first.

Michele: Getting back to re-channeling our sexual energy. Another great method is, that if you can't think of anything creative to do right this minute, to use your sexual energy for the positive, then try something physical like starting an exercise class, or going dancing, or simply taking for long walks. I know I feel that unification with spirit when I do this. Also, when taking deep breaths and breathing in the life force around you and into you, that is you! I like to breathe in through my nose and hold it for as long as I can, and then I slowly release the breath through my mouth. It really calms me down and gives me a feeling of well being and balance. Mediation is so wonderful for this as well. Oh my gosh Wilma, I can't believe it! Well I can, isn't that beautiful... just over there is a young couple in love, kissing passionately. Wow! They are just sitting there staring into each others eyes! How beautiful...thank you God for amore! This is what we are talking about... Yes! When there is Love involved, there is Spiritual Unification!! So now, let us affirm that for ourselves.

Sexual Unification

Dear Infinite Love, I am unified with Thee, knowing I am One with the Universe and that we are all interconnected. I now know that I am unified with your dear Infinite Love during sex and that sex is a spiritual expression of your loving creative energy that lives in me as me. This is the creative energy of the Universe. I am present for my partner and unify this experience with love and with all of my heart.

I now know my partner is a reflection of myself. I pay attention to my partner's loving spirit, so that we both feel the unification of your Divine blessings. I stay in peace and harmony with my partner.

I thank you Infinite Love for this awareness. I release this to the Infinite within, knowing that all is joyful, loving and beautiful.

And so it is.

Notes

Sex

1. What is the creative energy of all geniuses?

2. How is sex spiritual?

3. Why is it important to be passionate?

4. What is sexual unification?

5. List four other reasons that you want to share a relationship besides good sex.

6. Why is it good to be celibate for a period of time?

7. What can you learn in a relationship when you are angry, sad, joyful etc.?

"The power to move in
this world is in your
subconscious mind."

-William James

Mind & Consciousness

Michele: Everything in life that is created in our physical world by us begins with a thought, an idea...even the chairs we are sitting on. This chair began in somebody's mind and Voila! A chair! It was designed and manufactured; the action was taken. Our thoughts create our physical reality. We are responsible also, for what occurs in our own experience through our very own thoughts. As Napoleon Hill said, "Thoughts are things." That is the big secret that so many people try to uncover about success, abundance and so much more. When you hear people say, "Change your thoughts and change your life," take heed! This is not New Age mumbo jumbo, and I even think the term "New Age" is rubbish as these thoughts have been taught to us for many centuries and by so many awake individuals. A lot of people get caught up in fear and say, "Oh my gosh, that's a scary thought! I am responsible for everything in my life!" Yes, we are! However, the beautiful side of it is, you can also take responsibility for all the good that you are creating in your life. Now that is a wonderful thought... Another thing I used to be concerned about was...all those negative thoughts. Does this mean that they are all going to be created into negative experiences now? Yes, and no.... When we wake up, we can stop the so called bad stuff, NOW! Yes, kick it goodbye. Begin today, right now, by saying, "The past is gone; I begin a new thought, and this thought is now being created in my reality. I forgive myself for the past. (See Forgiveness chapter) Today is a new day, and I begin today anew. There is no way, and no how that any negativity can now come upon me because the positivity overwhelms it, in goodness and in light. So today, from right now, I am born again. I start again with newness. The past negatives cannot affect me today. I only create in this moment goodness, prosperity, and wonderful relationships in all the multi-dimensional abundances in my life...in all of those beautiful areas of my life." You see, when situations come up that appear to be challenging, I respond, rather than react, and I allow myself to be guided by God, so that all right outcomes do appear. It does however, begin right here and right now with me.

Wilma: Michele, there are times that I think those good thoughts, and yet, the bad stuff still keeps turning up. Why is that?

Michele: Well, that's because we are still raising our awareness. Until we get to the point where we are continually affirming, to where we get to the point when we are not creating any more of that. Plus, when we change our response, things then look different to us...like something from the past that caused us so much stress. When we change our attitude, we literally can then see the good, and look for the solution rather than wallowing in the notion, "Oh, how did I create this?" Get out of that victim mode! Take positive action and put a smile on your face and keep on going! We will ultimately get to the point where everything feels in harmony, and eventually more and more good will come into our lives because that was exactly what we were expecting! Now we can experience everything that happens to us as an adventure that we can use and rise above! While we are still here in a physical body, we know we still have work to do, so our challenges are all gifts from the Divine... It is simply how we respond. The beauty of it all is so amazing. I do love life! I know the past is the past, and the present is now. Life is totally worth living to the fullest. Even though my life is beautiful now, there are many things that I want to achieve, and I wish to raise my awareness even more. There are so many things! I continuously say, "I am honest, I am open, I am fearless, I have faith. I know that all good is here now and I forgive myself for the past, knowing that now I am creating all new and good in my life."

Wilma: I find that this takes time and discipline and only then does faith become stronger. There have been a few people who have this deep conscience awareness, and then "Boom!" It can happen right away. Well, it can happen right away for some people. However, for me, I have found that it's like turning the QEII ocean liner around; you turn it bit by bit, and continue to work on it daily, staying on course and in the right direction. There are things, I find, that pull me off course. However, it is easier to get back on track, once I know how. The other challenge that I found, is that the people around us may not be supportive when they know that we are thinking in a different way from them. They say, "Well, that's not possible, you can't do that!" Just say "NEXT!" to such thinking (to yourself, of course)(laughing). Know that what you're doing is right because you have consciousness to do it. The "collective unconsciousness" of all of the thoughts of everyone else cannot pull you back if you are persistent. So I just stay on course, not caring to be part of the so called "norm," because people think the norm is to think like everyone else, and that is absolutely not true. More things have been done in this world...in fact, everything of any significance has been done by just a few people thinking for themselves. It takes only a few people to change a course, and if you look back on the planet's history, at inventions and new ideas, these are just a few people who have made big differences in the world. As an example, people thought the Wright Brothers were crazy. All one has to do is look uptoward the sky to see what good came from their so-called crazy ideas about a flying machine. It really is so important to stay away from the common thought...the "collective unconscious."

Michele: Wilma, to me, the "common thought" is no thought at all. It is just a regurgitation of all past events, there being not really any new original thoughts to be found in that lot. You know, I love thinking of the Wright Brothers and how people today think they have a fear of flying. Can we even imagine how the Wright Brothers felt? People thought they were crazy and they continued to literally risk their own lives every time they attempted yet another flight. I also think of Benjamin Franklin and also many others in today's society. My goodness, what about Steve Jobs who started Apple Computer! Look at all the wonderful minds that are alive and well in today's society. That is why I love the so-called "crazy thinkers." These people know about persistence; they are resilient. They didn't listen when people said to them, "It can't be done," and none of us have to listen either! Let's all be free thinkers and make our own choices in life-not somebody else's. So, let's all stay on track, keep our minds focused, and our consciousness true to our vision. It's so important to stay on track, and keep positive thoughts to yourself. One doesn't have to run around proclaiming, "Oh, I'm positive! You're being negative; don't be negative!" Just think about you, not them. People just get into fear, and that's okay. We all get into fear sometimes, but we can change that fear with our thinking. Napoleon Hill said, "Thoughts are things." Feel the fear, and do it anyway! And I love when Bob Proctor says "Do it scared, but do it!"

Wilma: Yes, do it scared but DO IT! I love that saying!

Michele: Me too! So let's change our thinking today. Let's get into a wonderful mind of clear consciousness-ageless and timeless, by immersing ourselves in new, more beneficial thought processes!

Mind and Consciousness

*The past is gone. I begin a new thought. This
thought is now being created in my reality.
I forgive myself for the past. Today is a new day
and I begin today with all of the love and faith in
the world. There is no way, and no how that any
negativity can come upon me because my
positivity overwhelms it in goodness and in light.
So today, from right now, I am born again; I
start again with newness. The past negatives
cannot affect me today. I only create in this
moment goodness, prosperity, health, happiness
and wonderful relationships. I experience all the
multi-dimensional abundance in my life right now
in a never-ending cycle of increase and
enjoyment.*

And so it is.

Notes

The Mind

Remember if you do not have the answers to these questions, take a nice deep breath and read through the chapter again.

1. What is the "big secret" that people try to uncover about success and abundance?

2. What does "change your thoughts change your life" mean?

3. How can you take responsibility for all that happens in your life?

4. How can you respond rather than react?

5. What if you begin to think good thoughts and so call bad experiences still seem to appear? What does this mean?

6. What is the collective unconscious?

7. Name some things in your life you would like to do and feel too scared to do it.

8. Make a written commitment that you will now break through the terror barrier and begin to do the things that scare you. Make sure these things are harming no one. In fact only do the things on your list that will help you in a positive way.

9. Speak out loud the mind affirmation at the end of this chapter three times a day for thirty days-your life will profoundly change for the better.

"When we give thanks
for all the things
we have to be
grateful for,
there are more and
more things created to be
grateful for."

Gratitude

Wilma: Gratitude is so important. Each time a little bit of good happens-just the slightest bit, I always say, "Thank you, God!" Every day I say for what I'm grateful. There were times earlier on, when I was just so upset that I couldn't function from all the stuff that was going on around me. The best way I could shift was to start thinking for what I'm grateful, starting with the tiniest little thing. I would think of one little thing and keep building on it and building on it. With gratitude, I would thank God for the good in my life. Now there are more and more things for me to be grateful for... I am in the flow. Gratitude actually helps me feel my unification with God. When I'm in gratitude, I know that I am totally One and I am so thankful. Oh my goodness, Michele, a porpoise just jumped out of the ocean! This is so neat-as we discuss gratitude, porpoises are leaping out of the sea! I've never seen that before... that was so beautiful....(sighs). Anyway, where was I? By unifying myself with the creative power of the universe and by putting myself in the flow keeps me in the flow. That is gratitude is to me-just a little bit of it.... I can't even explain it; it is such a strong emotion!

Michele: Yes sweetie, it's that feeling of heart glow, the feeling that all is well when we are truly grateful. I'm reading a book now, by Christopher Reeves, the actor. It's called, "Still Me." Here is this man, now a quadriplegic, on a breathing apparatus, and he's talking about all the things for which he is grateful and about all the wonderful blessings in his life. How many millions of people is he inspiring today to be grateful? What a wonderful message he is giving to the world! My very good friend, Gene Mitchener, the comedian, has muscular dystrophy, and he's also on a breathing apparatus. He has been in a wheel chair for most of his life, and he's always talking about joy and happiness and looking at the good in life! He teaches us all to not take life too seriously and to find the joy and fun in life. What an inspiration he is!! I highly recommend his books and audio tapes. Actually, I highly recommend any author's books or tapes that we have mentioned in this book. These are truly life-changing products! For me, these tools are what I consistently use to remind me of what CAN be done instead of what can't be done and to realize how blessed we all are! We have life; we are living and breathing. We don't have to think about from where our next breath comes, and even though Christopher and Gene do, they still live in their joy and embrace gratitude in their lives. They are such an inspiration to me! It makes me realize humbly how blessed I am.

Wilma: I know you don't like talking about it, but you went through a major car accident, Michele. You are my bionic girlfriend with all of the steel in your body. Is that when you started being grateful for life as well?

Michele: Well no, not straight away. I felt very sorry for myself, and at first, I was a terrible patient. Gosh, those doctors and especially the nurses deserve a medal for bravery (laughing). I am very grateful now. How many people get to walk again after something like that-let alone dance, roller blade and everything that I do? I truly am so very grateful for all that I have, and for all that I am achieving in my life. I love it all! It's like you were saying before, in another one of our conversations-remembering the beautiful bed in which I sleep. I'm so grateful for the comfort of that bed...and all the other little things. Even the person who invented Earl Grey tea...I love my cup of Earl Grey tea!

Wilma: You sure do, I even stock it in my house now... for when you come to visit. (Laughs)

Michele: Oh, and you even remembered to bring me back some Vegemite when you went to my homeland, Downunder. You are such a thoughtful person. When I'm not in alignment Wilma... and you've reminded me of this many times... I know I need to make a list of what I'm grateful for now. Writing it down helps me tremendously. I am so thankful that I have my health, my friends, my beautiful, caring, loving family, my life, my career, my wonderful team at MusiVation™, Jesse, Jennifer, Sue, Michael, Cindy and so many other amazing people in my life . I love to just get into the abundance in nature-the grass and the trees. There is abundance everywhere! You know, you can walk through the botanical gardens or some beautiful park... anyone can do that... and enjoy the beauty of nature. There is so much for which to be thankful! The more we are thankful, the more good we create and the more good we can see.

Wilma: As a practitioner in my church, one of the first things that we learn in order to have someone shift when they are really upset is to have them write down a gratitude list. It is interesting how quickly a person can shift when they go into gratitude mode. This is an actual cure for depression, being grateful every day. I find that with depression, somebody is so full of pain and so withdrawn that they can't see past the nose on their face. This exercise pulls them out of their funk and focuses their attention on all the beauty around them, rather than on themselves.

Michele: Wilma, right now I am so thankful for you. I thank you so much for being in my life and being my friend, and when I've gone through challenges in any form, you've been there for me-strong and supportive. I am so grateful to you for being here now and having this conversation. It clears so much. You are someone with whom I've always been able to be myself, and you've loved me unconditionally through the good and the so-called bad. I am so thankful to you my darling, darling friend, Wilma.

Wilma: You are such a darling friend too Michele!. It has been easy being your friend; it is just so natural. I love you very much! I am so grateful for you; you have really helped expand my thoughts. You just kept encouraging me and pointing out my talents and my gifts. At first, I didn't want to believe it. I was thinking, "Yeah, yeah, she is just being nice; she is just saying that!" Now, there are other people who are pointing out my talents as well, and I think, "Oh, I guess Michele was right!" You have been such a delight in my life...you are just such a beautiful person! Always upbeat, even when you were going through your challenges, you would bounce back up again. It is so delightful just being in your company and having our wonderful conversations together!

Michele: Oh, wow! You know what? I have to be able to say, "Thank you," and accept that. Thank you, thank you, Wilma. Me acknowledging you, and you acknowledging me-now that's true friendship. I know that I would not have attracted such a true friend unless I was able to be a good friend too. That's what it is all about. And, I had to learn to be a good friend to myself first. Sometimes, if I hadn't forgiven myself enough for something, that's when I realized I was not attracting the sort of really deep friendships in my life that I desired so much. I can think of many things in my past where I wasn't happy with how I handled those situations in business and in my personal life. I know, however, that now, I am doing all I can, and allowing Spirit to guide me, to make amends. Also, I am able to be there for the people that have been there for me. It was my unwanted fear that I allowed to take over me, and I knew that I first had to acknowledge that it was O.K. to feel the fear to then be able to work through it and to never deny it. There is no need for me to be like that any more. That's why my life is evolving into such a beautiful, happy, joyful, healthy existence now. That's why I'm so blessed to attract good friends into my life. You are the most wonderful person that I know; It's such a blessing! We do mirror back to each other. When someone would be saying something negative to me, that was something already within myself. That's why it's so important to stop and get out of that vibration and be grateful....grateful for the nose on my face with which I can breathe, grateful for the good in my own body, in my own health and in my life, grateful for anything precious. You are so right Wilma; it's the best thing in the world because when we get into a depression, we are totally immersed in our own egos. We are totally focusing on ourselves and the bad, for example, we say, "I'm not lucky in love. I'm not pretty enough. I'm not enough this or that!" On and on it goes like an old scratched record!! NEXT!!!! (laughing) Someone might be blessed enough to have six toes instead of five, for instance, but instead of saying, "Oh, I've got abnormal feet," say, "Gosh, I am blessed that I've got extra toes!"

It's a pretty bizarre thought, but it's so important to say "Thank you"! It's important for us to remember when someone is thankful to us as well and to be able to accept that. When someone gives us a compliment, we can return gratitude by saying, "Thank you!" instead of, "Oh, this old blouse? I just borrowed it." If someone gives you a compliment about your dress or whatever your attribute, then just simply, no matter what you're thinking, acknowledge that person by saying two beautiful and powerful little words, "Thank you!"

Wilma: You are so right! In my experience, when I give a compliment to someone, and then they pitch it right back at me, it tells me that they are not worthy of it. This dissipates the joy that I was receiving through the giving of the compliment. That's why it is so important, not only for yourself, but for the other person, to be accepting. Honor yourself, and honor who you are, and cherish all the gifts that you have. Be grateful for those gifts. When you are able to share your gifts, other people become grateful for your gifts as well. Hence, the gratitude circle is kept flowing, that positive energy going.

Michele: I love the team of people with whom I work, they are so wonderful. They have had so much faith in what we are doing and in the big vision. Jesse is so wonderful. I remember one day I said to him, "Thank you Jesse for doing that; that was wonderful!" He said, "Well, there is no need to say thank you; that is what I was supposed to do." I replied, "But I'm grateful that you did it, you did it so well, and you did it so beautifully!". I was sincere. Despite one thinking that one is "supposed to" do something, I think it is especially important to thank them for it! You might have hired a teenager to mow the lawn and told them, "Thank you for mowing the lawn; you did a great job." He might respond, "Well, you hired me to do it, no need to say thank you." You could then say, "I'm really grateful that you were here to do it; you enabled me to do other chores, and now that you are finished, we are all blessed!"

Wilma: That reminds me of my assistant, Sandy, a delightful, beautiful individual. I always write on the outside of her pay envelope, "Thank you for a great job," and then I draw the universal smiley face. Once, I was in a hurry and I put her check in the envelope, gave it to her, and said quickly "Thank you." "Wilma, you forgot the smiley face," she rattled. (I thought that was so darling that I took it back and put the smiley face on).☺ Even though you are paying people to work for you, it's so important to thank them. When you show appreciation often, they continue to love their job and enjoy working for you. It's really neat to thank them and surprise them, by doing little things that they don't expect. It doesn't take very much. It's just some little "thank you" to help them feel good about their hard work and about themselves! I think that is so much fun to do-to surprise people with little thank you's that are totally unexpected.

Michele: Yes! people are usually shown gratitude only on birthdays, anniversaries and special holidays. Doing it at a time when they are not expecting it is fun! This is so wonderful because it's reminding me.... for those people out there that work alone often, like I do, such as when I'm writing a song or I'm working in my home office....Sometimes, it's a challenge to get self-motivated, and the minute I feel this way, I stop, and say, "Thank you God!" Thank you God for this day, thank you God for this moment, thank you God for this roof over my head, thank you God for the wonderful environment where I live and for my wonderful country, Australia, and for America, and Malaysia, and for all the beautiful countries in which I work, live and play. Just simply: THANK YOU GOD!!!" And then I put on my positive music or a James Brown tape, and I am immediately and instantly swept into a new, higher vibration. Fun and positive music puts us into an immediate "up" vibration! Without even knowing it, you will be smiling and dancing around! Look in the mirror, right where you are, right now. Put down this book and look in the mirror...make-up or no make-up, teeth or no teeth, and smile. Smile at yourself! You will feel happier instantly. Then say, "Thank you, (your name)!" Just smile, and you will feel so good! It is a fun activity to try when you are not feeling particularly grateful about things. So now, we are going to give thanks and greet the day with love in our hearts.

Gratitude

I greet this day with love in my heart!
I am living this day as if it were my last.
Today, I begin anew day, today
I have a new start.
I am grateful for this day and all the good
I have and all the good that keeps flowing to me
in a never ending cycle of increase
and enjoyment.
I know that all I could ever need or desire is
supplied to me from the One source,
The Infinite God.
So, Thank you life for this day, and for my
beautiful, happy, prosperous and passionate life!

And so it is

Notes

Gratitude

Remember if you do not have the answers to these questions,
take a nice deep breath and read through the chapter again.

1. Write down why gratitude is important in your life.

2. Write down 20 things for which you are grateful.

3. This week, share with 3 people for what you are grateful in your life, including them. Write down their names now.

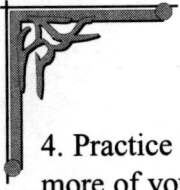

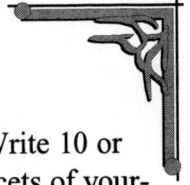

4. Practice honoring yourself and who you are. Write 10 or more of your attributes and why you like these facets of yourself.

5. Look in the mirror, smile and say, "I love You, Thank You!"

6. When you go to sleep at night, thank your higher power for all that you are grateful

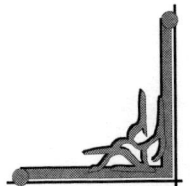

"Judge not, that ye be not judged. For with what judgement ye judge, ye shall be judged."

The Holy Bible
(Matthew 7:1)

Judgement

Michele: Wilma, all I know is, if I am judging another person in a negative way, then it's because there is something there that I recognize about myself, and I have to stop and look at that. The best way I can think of explaining it is through a humorous analogy. I mean, how do we know that we feel like eating a piece of chocolate unless we have already experienced the taste? So, how could I know someone is doing something I think is negative unless I have experienced that same thing within myself? We all have a shadow side. There is no point in denying this; we simply have to know this and move on with choices that are good for us. I think it is important to know this about others as well.

Wilma: Chocolate, huh! You know, I don't think I've even seen you eat a piece of chocolate. (laughing) Go on girl, this is great. Different, but great none-the-less.

Michele: Well, I have no right to give my opinion to another human being about them. It's like someone was saying, "Oh, this critic wrote this really rotten stuff about an acting friend of mine." I said, that's why they are called "critics." Remember, if you believe the good stuff people say, you also have to believe the bad stuff too. That it is why it is so important to learn how to make our own life decisions, feel good about them and not doubt them. You know that deep within yourself, you do not need another person's approval or opinion. Of course, we have to judge some things in life, such as checking the traffic when we cross the street, but, as much as we can regarding "judging others" let's say "NEXT!" Remember what Napoleon Hill said, "If you are wanting to speak of another negatively, write it in the sand on the sea shore and let the waves wash it away." I know I've said this before when we talked about forgiveness; it's such a great way to think. By the time we drove to the beach, we probably would not feel that way anymore.

Wilma: Especially if you live in Texas (laughing)!

Michele: (laughs) You are funny today! I am trying to stay focused, so enough seriousness...okay? Let's hear from Wilma!

Wilma: Not judging or being nonjudgmental, or even better yet, judging right...is so hard for me. It is something I work on every-day, because it's so easy to judge people! To judge how they look, what they are wearing, what they are saying...well...it should be this way or that way. That is so hard. Remember those three little Buddhas that you gave me; Hear no evil, Speak no evil, and See no evil...they are so neat! To me, they are a constant reminder because the "evil" is the judgement. As you said Michele, it is something inside that a person doesn't like about himself or herself. Also, all around us all the time, on TV, with our friends, just everywhere...we are surrounded by negative judgement. To keep our focus and to emphasize right judgement, meaning looking at the good in all things....now THAT is judging "right!" I have to keep bringing myself back and bringing myself back, by focusing on right judgment. That's been the hardest thing for me to do. However, every day, I do get better at it.

Michele: That is so funny...I mean, in this day and age, people even judge a man by the size of his penis. Yes, I said the word penis! If this word triggers you and you think that I am being naughty, well the word "ear" or "leg" should also trigger you. It is simply a part of our beautiful anatomy that God created (and well, some people also judge the size of our ears)!

Wilma: Okay, Michele is back to her unusual analogies and also making a very good point (laughing).

Michele: I mean seriously, Wilma have you ever read the rubbish that they are feeding young minds about sex? Phew, it is so negative! You know, it must be so challenging being a young man in this day and age. Wow, am I judging?

Wilma: Michele, this is OK. You are not judging another; you are allowed to have an opinion about world issues, and this is an issue for men, I guess. I bet it is just as challenging for women concerned about being the right weight and all that other stuff with which young women's minds are being filled and so, it works both ways.

Michele: You are so right. There are many sides to every story and that is what each soul chooses to experience when they decide to be born into this era. It is a very exciting time to be alive with the new Millennium and yes, I can see it now. I can see good all around. As we say in Australia, "Goodonya mate for turning me around!" Wow, just discussing the word "judgement" can get us into, what else.... Judgment (laughs). We've got to get to know people better which reminds me of Howard Jones' great song, "Like to get to know you well, so we can be one together." Anyway, the only way we can do that is to open our hearts and our minds and get to really know people in a deeper, less superficial way. It's so challenging to be like that. We can at least acknowledge and be aware of this way of thinking when we are judging. We must, at least, be able to stop, and say, "What's this all about? Why am I judging that person?" There are so many types of judgment. I can say, "That person is a really good person because they have done that." Well, that's my opinion, but at least I've said it to myself. It's my opinion about it. I'm allowed my opinion, but I've got to remember to stay on track and only judge what's good for me and what's acceptable to me.

Wilma: That is a good point, and remind me to get a Howard Jones CD; It sounds like his lyrics are right on!

Michele: I will; and yes, Howard is so right on and positive, see? That is my opinion. I can look at someone, for example, and say, as we were discussing earlier, "Okay, my judgement, for me, is what I want to create." I can't say that what another person is doing is "right" or "wrong" because that is none of my business. What I can say, however, is that it is not acceptable to me or for me to judge, at this stage of my evolution. Only then can we move on, staying in our own world and away from other people's opinions. It almost gets to me, Wilma. It's so funny; if a critic writes something up about a movie, then moviegoers can be greatly influenced by one opinion. It's like "The Matrix." I thought that this was an amazing mind-shifting movie that taught us to not be followers, to trust in our own intuition and break through this mind-coma collective rubbish! And then there's all this negative stuff from the critics. The critics tell us that the long black coats the actors wore in the movie were a negative influence on children. After the shootings in Colorado, I understand why people become worried. However, it was not the coats that screwed up those angry youths' thinking. Who knows what was going on in those young minds! It sure wasn't fashion. There were, however, so many great things about that movie that taught us about getting out of the paradigm of what the rest of the world believes is their "dream time." Literally snapping or breaking yourself free from the consciousness of everybody else, diving into your own consciousness and into the infinite consciousness was the movie's theme. The only way to accomplish this is to stop judging what other people are doing. It is so challenging for me as well; at least I am aware of it. If a person wants to do this or that, it's their business...as long as it's not hurting my life. I know that attitude can seem selfish and as if you don't care what happens to other people....but of course I care; I care deeply, and yet, it's none of my business. If I choose to improve the rainforest, well, that's my business. But if I don't choose to do so, then that's my business too.

Wilma: It's also so easy to judge ourselves and to be critical of ourselves. We've got to eliminate that kind of thinking from our thoughts. This has been very, very challenging for me as I have to keep going back and shifting those thoughts. Saying that is not the truth about me. The truth is, "I am!" I affirm that "I am a beautiful, spiritual Being." I found that I would, knock myself for the things that I've done, or didn't do, or should have done...the shoulda, woulda, coulda's. I have found it much easier to get the shoulda, woulda, coulda's out of my life.

Michele: We have no right to give our opinion about other people or their lives. We have no right to judge anybody; it's all about who we are. It's so challenging sometimes because we say, "Oh, that person should do this." You know that old saying, "Don't should on people (laughing)." What do we know? The person who's working at the gas pump may be some great sage or angel who is experiencing that particular job in this lifetime. He pumps gas and assists the world by shining his light. We don't know. If someone comes to us and they want to learn or talk about a topic, then that's different. We have no right to judge because we don't know...only God knows. I love, as you know, Stuart Wilde; he is so awesome! I love what he says when people ask for his opinion. He says, "Well, I don't have an opinion about that." People look at him and say, "What do you mean you don't have an opinion; you must have some judgement about it." He replies, "No, I don't have any specific judgement or opinion about that." It freaks people out. I love it...absolutely love it!

Wilma: He is different! You know Michele, I also had to change some things I was doing with my time. I had been volunteering on an arbitration committee, and I had to judge people on their ethics, whether they did something good or bad. I thought I did this to get myself in alignment, and yet I found it much easier to simply not be on that panel. I volunteered to do other things. While I was arbitrating, I was not in alignment with my thinking. Now, what I'd like to do and for which I have volunteered is to become a mediator. Through a mediator, people can arrive at a mutually beneficial agreement rather than simply judge who's right or wrong.

Michele: That's great, Wilma! You are negotiating to help people communicate together. It's all about communication. Why do people go to therapists? When you say to a therapist, "What do you think?"... they may respond, "Well, what do you think?" It's about what we think. Most people don't really think. What we are actually doing is simply going over and over old issues; we need to think new thoughts. Judging brings us back to our thoughts of the past. I go to a spiritual practitioner. She assists me in acknowledging fear and helps me work through it, and then we affirm the truth. This is what I love. She is so solid in her faith! We must learn, however, to not stay stuck in the past. You know what was great for me Wilma? I lived in Malaysia for three years, and when I first went there, it was really challenging for me as it is mostly a Moslem country. The Moslem women....oh gosh, I thought, it must be so hard for them. Their gender role seemed so negative until I met some deeply spiritually-involved Moslem women. It is their religious choice, because in Malaysia, it's not like other strict Moslem countries where you have to dress all in black. Some of the women choose to do so, and some do not in Malaysia. Anyway, I met some wonderful people and families that made the religious decision themselves. They were totally into God because they had found the light. They had found their truth. Malaysia is such a beautiful country with so many wonderful, old deep beliefs that are awesome to study. There are Buddhist monks and Hindu priests and so many deeply spiritual people. I believe that when we start thinking with more of a positive attitude, it helps us become better sisters, brothers, mothers, Christians, Buddhists, or Moslems, etc. We all must follow our own spiritual path to achieve spiritual fulfillment in our lives. We must let people do their own thing as we are all at different levels of awareness. Each individual is exactly where one needs to be for one's unfolding, right now. Let's change ourselves first and not think that we have all the answers...because we don't! Anyway, living in Malaysia assisted me in getting out of my so-called western judgements. Before I went there, I just thought that all Moslem women must be in hell. How wrong I was! People come from different cultures and have different habits and upbringings, and I must respect that. We are all brought up differently, and we all have our own thoughts. Who am I to judge? Judge not, lest ye be judged!

Wilma: Wow, what a great learning experience for you! Travel is such a great way to learn about our planet and all of the different cultures.

Michele: And Wilma, the eastern countries REALLY have culture!

Most of the younger countries have borrowed from the cultures of other places. We can learn so much from older civilizations. Also on judging; I was just wondering how you know what's right for another person? I know that, for me, I went through a horrific experience with my car accident; but I had to go through that experience to get to where I am today. Sometimes we need to go through that stuff, whatever it is, until we see the light. Thank God we do not all need such a kick in the bum as I did! We cannot be in judgement, unless someone comes to us and says, "Help me! I want to get out of this negativity. Can you help me?" And then you can be there for them. If people haven't asked for help, how dare we try to preach our beliefs into them; it's none of our business!

Wilma: It doesn't do any good anyway.

Michele: Exactly, anybody who has children can relate to that.

Wilma: It does not do one bit of good to preach to anyone who has not asked for help. The best thing to do is to set a good example, and then people will come to you and ask for help. In my training at church as a practitioner, we are told not to walk up to someone and say, "Oh, it looks like you're having a problem today, I can help you with that." They have to ask for help. You can advertise your services, but they have to physically approach you and ask for the help, which incidentally, is actually a two-fold thing; one, because they are acknowledging that they need to change, and two, because they are brought on the right path for their growth.

Michele: We only know when we are ready. It's like trying to speak French to someone who doesn't speak French. Someone reading this book right now might be in judgement saying, "How can these two women be telling us anything?" We're not telling you anything; we are just sharing our own experiences as we always do together. If anybody enjoys this, great. If they don't, great. If someone gets into judgement mode and they become defensive, or if they are triggered by anything that is written here, then that is great. You can, at least, begin thinking to yourself....Why am I judging this? Why am I so critical of a particular thing, and why is it triggering me? Really stop and ask yourself! You will be so empowered by that...totally empowered.

Wilma: The best solution I find is to just be a good finder. Look for the good in all things and focus on that.

Michele: Let's focus on the good in everyone! As Terry Cole-Whittaker writes in her great book, "What Other People Think of Me is None of My Business," "What I like of me is my business and my business alone and I must only judge what I'm doing and better myself and raise my own awareness." Let's read a great affirmation now to acknowledge and to know; Judge not lest ye be judged!

Judgement

" Judge not that ye be not judged, for with what judgement ye judge, ye shall be judged"

I now know that judging others is merely the law of cause and effect. Nature and the Universe holds
nothing against anyone. I am judged by my own acts. Punishment and reward are reactions of the law of the Universe. If I wish to be happy, I know that I must choose my judgement to be good, happy and constructive. Then, I am making right use of the law of the Universe.

I am now a person who always chooses to see the good in others as I know we are all individuals on our own spiritual journey.
I choose to love others,
to be happy, healthy and to live in peace.

I am now happy and whole.

And So It Is

Notes

Judgement

Remember, if you do not have the answers to these questions,
take a nice deep breath and read through the chapter again.

1. Why is it important NOT to judge others?

2. Name some people you judged today. Why did you judge
them? Were they irritating you? Perhaps you didn't like the
way they looked?

3. Take a closer look at why you judged those people above.
Do some self-examining. Did it remind you of something in
your past? What did it feel like?

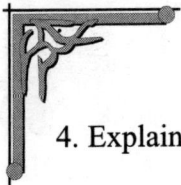

4. Explain what cause and effect means.

5. Practice seeing the good in others everyday. Be a "good finder."

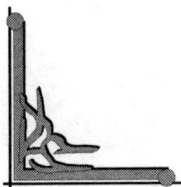

" Happiness must be based on an inward sense of security, a sense of belonging to life and to each other, a desire to give, to be kind and compassionate, and to be able to put ourselves in the other person's position. "

—Ernest Holmes

Happiness and Freedom

Wilma: With freedom comes happiness, and with happiness comes freedom. Which comes first? Actually, being clear about who you are and what you are, experiencing the moment of every day, living each moment fully and having all the good flow....this, to me, is happiness. There is so much joy when you see how the Infinite plays a major part; it's like dancing with the Infinite. There is so much harmony, beauty, and freedom. Everything in this Universe is interconnected. I call this the unified field, the unified field of vibration in everything. It's the vibration, which to me, is the creative power of the universe. It is God's voice; it's our connection with God. With this interconnection, we can attract so much good... once we are aware of it. Most people are not aware of this vibration and how we put our own, individual vibration out there. It's been tested with divining rods. You can walk up to a person who is sad or depressed, and these rods don't even move. You can go right up to them.

Michele: This is wonderful for those people who need proof!

Wilma: Yes, it's amazing and when the rods are tested on somebody who is ecstatically happy, they go "wang, wang, wang!"

Michele: That's great! It is the energy, the oscillation and the mass of vibration! In fact, it is a faster oscillation than vibration. It is so clear. When we reach that higher level of vibration, it is called happiness, and it shows right away. We attract, to ourselves, people that are in a similar speed of vibration. It is similar to when you walk up to a person and you are aware that they are depressed. You don't want to stay with them because they are not putting out the energy to which you are resonating, especially if you are feeling very exuberant as they are feeling down; you are not attracted to that flat energy. I simply put my energy out there and imagine that depressed person happy and joyful. We all get depressed sometimes so it's nice to let others know that someone is sending us love at those times. Once a person can really understand this fully, they can exert so much happiness onto the world because happiness actually comes from within. It's not anything external; it's all inside. By creating that higher vibration within, we can experience the joy and our connection to spirit. This gives us the freedom to do anything we choose.

Wilma: What is the difference in saying, "faster oscillation" as opposed to "higher vibration?"

Michele: I've found that people who are newly into metaphysics and various spiritual studies, pass judgement; sometimes subconsciously, and say, " I'm at a higher level of vibration than you, etc." They hint that somehow they may be better than others, and that is simply not the truth; it is simply ego. I feel that we're all operating at different frequencies or speeds. This is why the divining rod started vibrating when it was near the happy person; our vibrations are faster when we are happy. When we are not feeling so good, we are at a low oscillation or speed. It's a slower vibration if something is not going well. It doesn't mean that the person isn't spiritual or highly aware generally; it's only at that point in time. When we rate at a faster vibration, we tend to draw to us a lot of great good, and that is what it's all about. It's really wonderful because you can feel the energy. It's hot, it's wonderful! When I'm with you Wilma, you're always in such a great vibration; I can feel it immediately when I'm with you.

Wilma: Well ditto, my dear!

Michele: It's not that you can make me happy, but when I'm around you, it adds to my joy. No one can make us anything; no one can make us happy. That's impossible...however, people can add to our joy. If you feel good when you are with someone, you know that they are in good vibration. It's a good place to be... and it's freeing. It's our choice to be free, and it's our choice to not be around people who are always oscillating in that flat, non-pulsed way. If you could read their thoughts, they would tell a story....you would read their "I can't do it" and "There are limitations in life" thought patterns... NEXT!!! (Laughing)

Wilma: Happiness too, comes from the inside and is a continual process of trying to clear all of our negative thoughts, with the goal of assuming a completely different level of consciousness. Having the knowledge that, no matter what happens, all is well. Very few people can say that all is well. I think there is a quote by Emerson, "Few are the people that can say all is well." Happiness absolutely has to come from within. Nobody can give us happiness, and nothing can make us happy. We may be happy at first, like when we get something new and exciting for example, a car, a house, or a job promotion...of course, it's exciting to get stuff. Soon, the newness wears off, and we end up back where we were. Happiness is being able to maintain that continual glowing inside, paired with the understanding that all is well.

Michele: Happiness is a choice. As Abraham Lincoln once said, "People are as happy as they choose to be." We can choose to be happy.

Wilma: How can someone do that?

Michele: They make a decision to be happy. We can use affirmations and other tools to help us reprogram our marvelous minds to the positive. Sing it out loud, yell it, get it out and continuously reprogram your mind to happiness in all areas of your life. You will eventually cultivate multi-dimensional abundance and real happiness in your life. It is very freeing to be happy; happiness and freedom are yours right now! Take it! It is your choice!

Wilma: OK, I choose happiness! (laughing) See, it has worked already!

Happiness And Freedom

The purpose of my life is to be happy! My own
mental attitude is the most important influence in
my life, working with peace, joy and success.
I now choose to be happy! I choose to be free.
I think for myself. I allow The Infinite to guide
me in all that I do.

I have a right to any happiness of which I can
conceive, provided that it hurts no one and is in
keeping with the nature of Divine Law.
I know I must change the conditions within
myself to change the outer conditions in my life.
I now live with inner peace and know that I can
face all challenges with calm and reason because
I think happy thoughts. As Peter Pan said..............

" With just one happy thought , I can fly "

Notes

Happiness and Freedom

1. What does this mean "with freedom comes happiness" and "with happiness comes freedom"?

2. Why is it important for your energy to be at a faster oscillation?

3. How does it show in your physical world when your energy is at a faster oscillation?

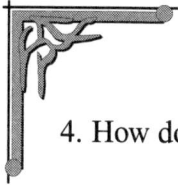

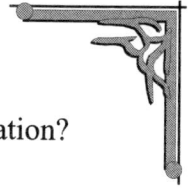

4. How do you get your energy to a faster oscillation?

5. Where does happiness come from?

6. What is the first step in being happy?

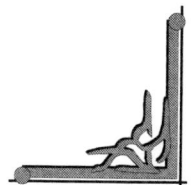

"In the attitude of silence, the soul finds the path in a clearer light, and what is elusive and deceptive resolves itself into crystal clearness."
-Mahatma Gandhi

Meditation

Wilma: Meditation has a different meaning for each person.. From somebody just going into space and contemplating, to the Buddhist who will spend weeks, even years, in meditation at extremely deep levels. So with meditation you can do with it, what works best for you. There are some people who like to meditate while sitting in a chair, some people prefer lying down and others like to sit in what is called the lotus position with the legs crossed in a certain fashion. To me, it's whatever works. I like to sit with my legs crossed and just clear my mind for about a half-hour. Sometimes it turns out to be longer than that and I ask for God to reveal Himself to me so that I am in touch with my Higher Power. In order to do that, I have to clear the chatter out of my mind and just breathe, concentrating on the breath or on words such as, "I am One with God". That is what I usually say and then I go into, "I am". That works best for me. When we are connected with God, or whatever we choose to call the Creative Power, The Infinite Presence, things become more and more clear. In fact it even helped my health as I used to have high blood pressure and that has now gone completely. I had allergies that also went away. I can not do a day without meditation. I just feel so connected when I do that and everything is in the flow when I am meditating. To start off, sometimes people just need to sit for five minutes or ten minutes; so just set a clock. That's how I started. I had a hard time being still at first. Now, it's such a wonderful freeing experience and earlier today, I was lying in the pool, floating and meditating. That was so wonderful just being....That to me is what meditating is all about. So what about you Michele, what is it to you?

Michele: Meditation to me is a wonderful thing, it is clearing our minds and allowing God to speak to us. There are many different ways of doing it like you said Wilma, it's really good to start with breathing through your nose and breathing out through your mouth to the count of five....Breathe in, holding the breath to the count of five and then completely release it. Breathing slows everything down and it helps you relax, relieving stress that the body has been

112

holding. I found when I was in so much horrific pain, after I got out of the hospital from my car accident, that deep breathing helped me so much when ever pain came up. So then, I started listening to creative visualization tapes, the first one being by Louise Hay, which started me with my breathing. It was a guided meditation, which really helped me because I still couldn't get the thoughts out of my head. It helped me slow down and I could listen to Louise guiding me.

Wilma: I also love her tapes.

Michele: Yes, she is very clear and her tape helped me tremendously. I still love guided meditation tapes. However, I also now at last, can have quiet meditation where I just still my mind. To me, the quiet comes after I've done a mind treatment, done my affirmations. This I call prayer, when the words have stopped and the answers and guidance come to us in the stillness; That is true prayer. Then I know, that all that I need to know will come to me, easily and effortlessly. I would say, at least five nights a week, I go to sleep listening to a guided meditation. Whether it's one of my own tapes or from somebody else. Whenever I hear anyone say, "Breathe" I go immediately into that peaceful state... Just breathe, it's so wonderful!

Wilma: I work just the opposite way. First, I will meditate and feel totally in touch with the Infinite. Then, I do my prayer treatments. That seems to work best for me and so you can see how different we all are! I feel for me, the meditation is the clearing and leaving the way open.

Michele: We're not trying to confuse any one here because this is just a conversation between two people. So, a lot of different people can relate to whatever works for them. Some people can get to that place simply by visiting a rose garden, staring at a rose and breathing in that scent. So do whatever works best for you! Let's begin now by simply breathing....

MEDITATION

I stop now and I take in three deep breaths and clear my mind to allow the peace and confidence that I know already exists within me.

(Say this silently to yourself)

First breath: "I breathe in peace..."(Count to five)... "I now breath out any tension."

Second breath: "I breathe in the confidence of who I really am. I am that I am.... I now breath out any doubts and fears."

Third breath: "I breathe in all the good the Universe has for me.... I now breathe out any negative thoughts from the collective unconscious....

I now stop and listen. I know that The Infinite is looking after me and guiding me to right action, right thinking and right opportunities.

All is well....

and so it is."

.........................BREATHE................ ●●●●●●●●●

Notes

Meditation

1. Why is meditation important?

2. Practice meditation if you are not already doing so. Sit comfortably for 10 minutes..set a timer if you wish. Use the breathing technique in the chapter. Practice clearing your mind by continuous breathing: Do this everyday increasing time by 5 minutes when you are ready..so that you can meditate for at least 20 - 30minutes a day. (If this is too challenging for you, we suggest utilizing a creative visualization tape from Michele's MusiVation™ catalog at the back of the book.)

"Success is the progressive

realization of a worthy ideal"

-Earl Nightingale

Success

Michele: Wow! I love that quote, "Success is the progressive realization of a worthy ideal." And James Allen said, "an ideal is an idea that we have fallen in love with." However, as you know Wilma, I prefer to say, "Have risen in love with." This is such a perfect definition of success...because it is in the journey when we grow in our spiritual awareness, when we have something so beautiful that it sometimes scares us. However, I love what Bob Proctor says, "If it doesn't scare you a little bit, then it is not big enough of a dream." I love that! Whatever your IT is...whether it's opening a restaurant, getting married, starting a singing or acting career....whatever your dream is, it will probably scare you a bit. Otherwise, it's just not worth doing if you're not going to grow from it and stretch the realm of possibilities. Oh, my goodness me! All I can say is, "I've been very scared!" I must be doing okay (laughing)!

Wilma: While on the subject of fear...I am aware that when I create an idea and feel fear, I do not run away from it. I embrace it and allow myself to be in it ...as if putting on a coat. I wrap myself up in it because I know that's exactly what I have to do. I know that it's just so right. Some fears that arise are rational fears that could be dangerous for you. Of course, don't do anything that could endanger your life. I am talking about that feeling of fear that is imagined and not real! In addition, with success, it is not the end, in itself, that counts. As Earl said, "it's the journey along the way that is so much fun to embrace." Once we achieve a goal, we tend to set another goal and another one, etc. So, we must have satisfaction in the experience of achieving our goals! Of course we must plan ahead, but we must also stay in the "moment of the doing"... like we are doing with this book.. We know we have a book to write as our current goal through these conversations, and it is so exciting!

Michele: ....And, we are just doing what we do, anyway! Again, I'm going recommend Bob Proctor's book, "You Were Born Rich."

It's such a great book, and Bob Proctor has been such a great teacher to both of us, Wilma. I remember what we talked about back in 1993... I said to him, "Bob, I really don't care about material stuff, about the beautiful houses and the cars and stuff, I just want to sing." Then he replied to me, "But Michele, you desires will raise your awareness. Write down that you want beautiful houses and all the niceties of life so that you will attract more and more success...to acquire what you desire." I understand this now. It doesn't mean that you have to buy the house; it just helps you raise your awareness when you are setting material goals. Some people just do not understand that. This has helped me to tremendously raise my awareness...and that's why creative visualization boards are good; one can write down all those affirmations. Success, for me, is getting out there and living my life and feeling fulfilled. That is success! I love when work and play are synergistic, so that you don't even know the difference between them. What we are doing right now Wilma, is a perfect example of this. We are sitting here on this beautiful balcony at this fabulous place in Mexico and are having an exhilirating conversation together about life... and, we are putting it into this wonderful book. I am enjoying the journey and living in the moment...just look at that beautiful ocean! Everybody can do it! I'm not thinking about anything else. I'm not thinking about the songs I'm writing for my new album or any other business. I am here, present in the moment. I think it's wise to refrain from sharing with people all of our visions and dreams because a lot of people would say, "Oh, you can't do that. What do you mean you're going to open a restaurant? You're not that great a cook/chef anyway." People can be cynical, but you can do it! You can do whatever it is that you desire. Also, I believe it's important to have a good business plan and then take action, and do it responsibly.

Wilma: I've acted irresponsibly in the past, and I know that it is not the way to do things. However, I learned. I learned a lot from those actions, and I don't regret ever doing it that way because, it was all that I knew at the time. You can learn from the mistakes you have made in the past. Those mistakes can really, really help you in the now.

Michele: Well then Wilma, they were not really "mistakes" because you did not repeat them; you learned from them. It was simply an educational experience....

Wilma: Yes! That is great way of looking at it! Most of the time, I hear people say about their jobs, "Oh, I can't wait until the day is over; or, what do you do to pass the time?" Pass the time? You only become older more quickly with this outlook. Experience the day! Experience the moment! Now that is when people are truly fulfilled. To me, I must live in the joy of each day and in the moment of everything that I do! Just experience it! Success is knowing that you can accomplish this.

Michele: Yes, only boring people can be bored (laughing)! It's so wonderful to see people stepping out and going beyond what we have learned at school, going beyond what we are doing now, knowing that nothing is impossible. All is possible, everything...there are no limitations in life. Success is so fulfilling when we revere the ride...no matter how bumpy it may be! Whatever success means to you and whatever fulfills you, for goodness sake, do that thing! For example, you may have a crush on someone, and you want to ask them out. Well then, ask them out! Only then are you successful, and you feel good. Even if they say, "No," then you are still considered successful because you had the guts and the nerve to ask them. It's not about what doesn't happen to you; it's about what you do. You're taking action; you're stepping out, and you're doing it. As a musician, I remember playing in cover bands (playing other people's music) and thinking, "All I want to play is my original music." But, at the very least, I was out there playing music and becoming better at my craft. Also, I was getting better at my technique, at performing and singing, until eventually, I got to the point where I could sing my originals songs and actually create money from that venue as well. So, it doesn't matter about the frustrations that happen along the way because those frustrations propel us to move forward. It's easy to feel a bit frustrated or challenged because then it makes us work harder to reach our goals. Feeling uncomfortable is beneficial because it moves us out of that comfort zone, the zone in which we don't give 100% effort. Ultimately, our awareness of our goals improves, and we can then reach for greatness! One I went to watch the admirable musician, Howard Jones, perform, and I was courageous enough to give him one of my CD's, some flowers and a letter inviting him to co-produce and sing a song with me. I wouldn't have done that a few years ago because I wouldn't have expected that he would actually do it. But this time, I knew that, whether he accepted or not, at least I would feel fulfilled with presenting my plan to him. I was scared when I did it; of course, he is a famous singer from England, one whom I admire so much. I now meet so many great people that I admire, including multi-billionaire, Richard Branson, from Virgin Atlantic. He had started a new record label, "V2," and I wanted to get my music to him. His autobiography, "How I Lost My Virginity," is a must-read for all those who desire to be inspired to success! He is such a down-to-earth, wonderful bloke, and I am now happy to report that I am speaking with his record label in London. A few years ago, I would have never dreamed that this was possible, and now all this is happening to me! I know for certain that, if it can happen to me, then it can happen for anybody.

Wilma: That is such a great story! I know how long you had been visualizing meeting Richard. It's wonderful to take chances...if that is what it feels like to you...a chance. The way to grow is to live in the unknown, to step out there with faith, knowing implicitly that it is all going to work out for your best good. It's when you have that solid feeling of faith behind you, that the real growth begins. It is living in the realm of unknown possibility. I don't mean to implore one to behave irrationally or have no plan of action.

Michele: You bet! After all, you're not going to walk on a high-wire without a safety net especially if you have no experience doing this sort of thing....

Wilma: Right! But it is important to have the faith and the knowledge that you are being guided along the right path; there is a special joy and satisfaction that you feel along the way. You just know that it's the right way to go.

Michele: Oh yes! Imagine if someone simply exclaimed, "Oh, I want to be an astronaut. I want to be an astronaut...I am now an astronaut, I am now an astronaut!" The affirmation, in itself, doesn't bring about the end result, but it can certainly propel you to take some action steps; i.e. going to college and studying to become a pilot, apply for a job at NASA, etc. All of your dreams can come to fruition. Anything is possible. However, we must first take action in order for dreams to materialize; otherwise, it is just wishful thinking.

Wilma: Setting that action in motion is so important, even if you take just one little step each day. If you are too fearful of taking the necessary action, then take the smallest action of which you can think...just to get the process started, to get that positive energy flowing in the right direction for you. Sometimes it takes just that, a baby step, to get the ball in motion. Enroll others who are close to you in your efforts, and enroll God, of course. Continue to ask for God's guidance.

Michele: So, know that, and never give up on your dreams! Everything can come to fruition. So, let's go ahead into an affirmative knowingness, into a prayer for success. "Success is the progressive realization of a worthy ideal....." So go for it!

Success Treatment

I absolutely know and feel God in my life as me and through me and all around me.. I know that God knows how to do everything. All I simply am required to do is to be still and listen to God's guidance and then take right action. I have faith knowing that God knows how to manifest my visions for my success into my physical reality. When I let God in my life, all is successful. All my dreams and my desires have come to fruition and all involved in my business are also prosperous and blessed with all that we do.. Everyone involved profits greatly because you God are my business partner. You God, are my banker. You God, are everything in my life. Everywhere I go, there is beauty and successful, like-minded, positive people. I see the good in everything; I see the success in everything; I feel successful, and I am successful. I absolutely know this is the truth in every area of my life. If I feel in fear of some action, I go ahead and do it and know that the action will dissipate the fear.....clearly seeing that fear is just an illusion. God did not plant an acorn simply hoping it would turn into an oak tree. God simply does it. The plants don't think, "Oh gosh, I hope I turn out to be an oak tree and not a pine tree, or a tulip, or a rose." They just grow. God thought it and it happened that the oak grew. All that I do grows and prospers as I think into the mind of God and about all goodness. I keep my mind focused on the Big Vision and let it beautifully unfold with ease and Grace.

You planted me God so that whereever I need to be to grow spiritually, I know I will be as thy will be done. I am so thankful to you God. I do not have to ever think about whether or not my dreams are coming true. For what needs to be grown to accomplish my highest good, let it grow... and that which is not for my highest good be weeded out forever. I now come to a place of plenty, and all my blossoms are here, beautiful to behold for I am one with The Infinite. I am so happy! I love being successful and I am grounded in my success. I love the prosperity success brings to me. I love the successful, happy people that I now attract into my life. It is a joy and a blessing to be Your vehicle God, in all of this good.

I know that all people involved benefit through my success. I am here to be of service and to make a difference; I do this with God as my partner. Peace, Harmony, Beauty, Joy, Love, Health, Like-Minded Friends and Abundance are here now. I now release and let go of these words, with the knowledge that all was done before I even spoke a word. I have faith. Thank you God for my success!

Notes

Success

1. What is your "it?"

2. Does "it" scare you? If not think bigger until it does.

3. What do you do when you feel the fear associated with doing something big and different?

4. Why is achieving goals not as important as "the journey?"

5. Make a creative visualization board. It's fun! Use a large cardboard bulletin display that you can purchase at any office supply store. Peruse magazines and cut out images that you desire to manifest in your life and then add your own positive affirmations.

6. Think of some actions and steps that you can take toward your dreams. Write them down and act on them NOW.

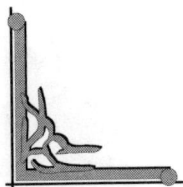

"Whatever the mind of man/woman can conceive and believe, it can achieve."

—Napoleon Hill

CAREER

Michele: "What are you going to do with your life when you grow up?" Wow! I know that many students must dislike those words because there are so many options. There are also a lot of options for people starting new careers especially if the job they have been doing for most of their lives leaves them feeling empty. It doesn't matter where you are right now; your career can be fulfilling and combined with success. A true career is doing something that you love to do. So, while you are on the path of seeing your career come to fruition and success, you can better handle the various challenges and frustrations that come along...if you love your career choice and what it is that you do. This means finding out what are your gifts and using those gifts that bring you joy into an income-producing activity. As you say Wilma, it's important to acknowledge our gifts, find a way to do the things we love doing, and then combine them into our career. For example, if you can't think of anything that you love doing more than dancing, and yet you are not that good at dancing...well, why not still find a way to be around dancing?

Perhaps you could enter into a partnership with someone, open a dance school, and hire great dance instructors. This way, you're still involved with dancing, getting lessons from professionals and making a living from it. You can make a career of anything...even if you're not experienced in it. If you have the desire, then you can d   o anything! Know this...if you have the desire, then it's because God has given you that desire to do it. It doesn't matter what it is; your career is so important. It's important to be able to know that you can do it, whatever it is. After all, we spend so much of our time in our careers! Also, it is vital that we have a great team of people to work with, if others must be involved. We can make sure that not only are they just good at what they do, but also, most importantly, they have a good attitude. I always bring it down to this. When you work with a team of people, for example, in a rock & roll band, you're as good as your worst player. You've all got to be in harmony, play the same music, and of course, be in the same key. So make certain that the people with whom you work are like-minded and that you feel really good with them, particularly if you are starting a business. I'm so blessed now. I've got Jennifer, Jesse, Sue and many other people who have come into my life. They are liked-minded individuals and extremely good at what they do. The bands in which I have sang have also had great players. I have only had one negative experience with a band member; he played great guitar but his attitude stunk. I never enjoyed playing with that band. After I stopped singing with him, my performances became even better, and we were all happier and more successful. We became more prolific, playing six nights a week to fantastic audiences all over the place.

Wilma: I didn't know that; I guess you just don't talk about and dwell on the past that much.

Michele: I prefer to live in the now. However, it is a good analogy for this topic. It's important for everyone to pull together, and if everyone with whom you are working are not like-minded, then go and find someone who is really at the top of their field or at least in your area of interest and ask them how they did it. Take them out for a cup of coffee, tell them how much you respect them, and ask for some advice. People who are successful in their career love to help others; they are honored to do it...trust me. This is how I met Richard Branson from Virgin. Remember, he started from scratch to begin Virgin Records and he also went on to own his own airline and so much more. It took a lot of action on my part to be able to meet him, and ultimately, I did. I know this type of positive thinking works well because I was able to keep my eye on the big picture and imagine that it had already happened. This is how I met Allan Phillips who is producing my new single. I also met Quino this way, the lead singer from Big Mountain. He sang on my new single. Now, I have to take action to get it distributed. Even though it looks like it will be with V2, Richard Branson's new record label, I am still leaving that to what is for my highest good. I totally trust in God as he knows what I desire, and for now, I am simply taking the action and letting the Universal flow let it happen.

Wilma: Taking that like-minded person out for a cup of coffee at first might be scary because you think, "Why would they want to talk to me?" However, I've found that the most successful people who love their work are the kind of people who are willing to share what they do. Those people who are mediocre are the ones that get caught up in that competition stuff and don't want to share. Sharing is the beauty of success, so go ahead and take this advice! I've been afraid to take people out for coffee in the past, but when I did, it was so nice. I was just amazed at how willing they were to share. I love how you finally met Richard Branson, impromptu in Chicago, without a prior meeting set up.

Michele: Yes I did that in a night club. God does work in fun ways. Richard was so wonderful to meet, however, I must say that he did know who I was, hence he was open to speaking with me. He knew of me because I had sent him so many things over the past six years, and I even showed up at his London office once. So, at unexpected hours, all our dreams do come to fruition. Now, let's discuss what a career is. If you don't know what it is that you desire to do with your life, you're doing something else in the interim, and you're not enjoying it, I suggest that the best thing to do is write down all of the things that you love to do. Then, say to the Infinite, "I absolutely know that I am now in my right career, doing what I love to do, and creating abundance in my life." The Universe will support us in what we love to do because when we are doing what we love to do, we are happier, healthier and attract more good into our lives. As I said before, when we are doing the things we love to do, it helps us get through the challenging times. There is nothing worse than hearing someone say, "I hate what I'm doing in my career!" By saying this, one attracts more of that, and their past becomes their future over and over again. However, don't give up totally and quit your present position on the spot, as you must continue to earn money for your rent and expenses.

Wilma: I am so glad you mentioned that. I found that I was not enjoying my career in real estate for a long time, and I was feeling so burned out. Then, I discovered that there were many parts of my job that I really did like... that I liked a whole lot. So, what I did was hire people to do the things that I didn't like to do and that which they loved to do. Now, I have a team that is working out very well. I get to do what I like to do, and I don't mind paying other people to do the other stuff. This way, I have made more money while everyone is happier. Our team has common goals and the process of changing the way we do business has been so much fun; it has resulted in lightening up many loads. I have also tripled my own income as a result.

Michele: My darling friend, as the years have gone by since we've known each other, I can say that you are truly living a life of multi-dimensional abundance. You are creating new and different things in your wonderful career. You're such a great success coach as well; all the people you are coaching are learning so much. You never even knew that you would be doing this. But now you're doing it and helping people... and we've also done this book together. The fact that you're living your dream gives me so much fulfillment, and I'm feeling blessed to be part of that dream. If you are reading this and you are in a career where you are successful, then go and help other people, and give them advice when they ask for it. Remember to allow others to do the work for themselves; you can't do it all. However, you can help them along the way through the sharing of your own experiences. We are all here on the planet to do our own thing. Again, it is so fulfilling to give encouragement to other people, to invite them to live their dreams. This, in turn, helps you. Live your dream so that your career path is your God-given path to spiritual awareness and to goodness. Also, be responsible with it, and have an action plan, so that you are clear. Remember, don't talk to anybody and everybody about your dreams and your visions because a lot of people may not want you to move on and be successful, as they themselves are too scared to do so themselves. These people feel more comfortable if those around them stay at their level. Keep it to yourself! Read your affirmations daily, know that they are coming to fruition and, in this way, they are here now.

Wilma: As you were talking, I just became so overwhelmed with good. It is so powerful just to be able to do this book, to be able to share our dream with so many people. I am excited just being here ...and as we look out at the ocean, knowing that it is all God...knowing all the good there is....We truly are One with it all!

Michele: That is right, "Where two or more are gathered....."

Wilma: (smiling) Yes, and for us to be able to broadcast that and radiate these messages everywhere; it is so beautiful! I really feel that by doing this, I am on my path, my path for even more success. When we can feel this, it is multi-dimensional abundance...abundance of joy, peace, harmony, health and wealth. Being in the right career and being on the right path is fulfillment.

Michele: "Fulfillment...yes!" I love that word. You really feel your heart. It almost feels as if my rib cage comes apart, and my heart is just out there glowing. Feeling vulnerable isn't scary; it's good to open up...this is not being vulnerable. Opening your heart attracts all the good. I see so many competitive sales companies even in this day and age; it's totally unbelievable...but it still happens... they have this warlike mentality of: "Let's kill the competition!" This is crazy talk! We are all here together as a team. We must help each other sing the One Song because we are all connected. There is no such thing as "competition!" The only person with whom I ever want to compete, in order to better myself, is me. The better I can become as a person at what I do, even though I know I still have so much to learn, is for what I strive. There are some days when I'll say, "Gosh, I thought I've come so far, but what am I doing in this negative vibration today?" At least I know that I am in a negative vibration! Before, I didn't even know when I was ...and that was scary. Now, when I know that I am in a negative vibration, I can snap myself out of it by saying, "Okay, I need to stop!" This aligns myself, gets me back on my path and allows me to SMILE! We must also remember not to have too many baskets. This will diffuse our energy. Start with one basket and fill that up to where it is healthy and prosperous. My eggs are all in one basket...the basket of what I love to do, i.e. self-improvement and music. It would be good to ask yourself, "Do I have too many baskets floating around?" After all, you don't want to become a basket case (laughing)! At the same time, it is important for me to focus on what I love to do and not become sidetracked by other things that are going on in other people's baskets.

Wilma: The conversation about competition reminded me of my business, the real estate business. People in this business talk about competition all the time. I hear, "Oh, you are competing for this and competing for that," and I reply, "No, I'm not because the business comes to me. I'm not competing with anyone." If you can make it greater, then you can always make more out of it. There is so much good...there is no limit to how much good can come to you from all different directions. Visualize a pie and imagine the so-called competition trying to slice up this one little pie. Now make that pie larger, so that everybody can have what they want out of it. It is so wonderful to be able to do that, to see no limits. Competition is so limiting to one's thoughts; one must see that there is such an abundance of everything out there!

Michele: Very cool idea! I like that. In fact, your idea ignited my appetite....Let's go eat (both laughing)!

Career

There are no limitations to my mind except those I
acknowledge.

I now acknowledge that I am a Powerful Spirit, having a
physical experience and therefore know that all things are
possible for me. I no longer dwell on my past so-called
mistakes, or what I believed were my limitations. I am One
with The Infinite. Therefore, I repudiate all thoughts of, "I
can not do it..." to... " I CAN DO IT!"

I was given desires to improve my life. I was given the
ability to achieve whatever I can dream. I love to work, to
serve and to build. My business expresses me, as I
express the business of life. I live life to the fullest, knowing that I can always rely on God to guide me through any
challenge. I never give up. I am strong and I am resilient.
I persist, knowing that all good is here, now. My vocation
is the thing my thought propels me to do. I think thoughts
that propel me to succeed in all areas of my life.
I love what I do and I am a responsible, thoughtful,
caring person.

Thank you life for my perfect, prosperous,
fulfilling career, now!
And so it is.

Notes

Career

Remember, if you do not have the answers to these questions,
take a nice deep breath and read through the chapter again.

1. What is a true career?

2. What is your true career?

3. Explain how you are as good as your worst player.

4. Name some people with whom you would like to take to tea/coffee, someone with whom you could learn. OK, so do it now! Remember, you are only 3 to 4 phone calls away from any of them (ma☺be 5 to get to the Pope)!

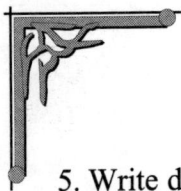

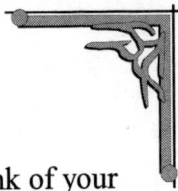

5. Write down all the things you love to do. Think of your passions! How can you use them in your present job or career?

6. What is multi-dimensional abundance?

7. What is fulfillment to you?

8. Why is competition limiting?

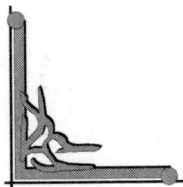

" When the act of reflection takes
place in the mind when
we look at ourselves in the light
of thought we discover
our life is embosomed in
beauty "

Ralph Waldo Emerson

BEAUTY

Michele: I love that quote from Emerson on beauty! Another quote from Emerson about beauty that I love is, "Not in nature, but in man is all the beauty and worth he sees." In those days, the authors always said, "he," but we know what they mean is man, woman or human beings. Beauty is within; it really is, Wilma. There's beauty all around us, all the time, if we choose to see it. When you meet someone for the first time, you are in your old paradigm, your old way of thinking of perhaps how this person is not handsome or pretty, or whatever. And then, when you get to really know them, you are able to see that their beauty lies within, and that they are genuinely loving individuals. Their beauty now shows on the outside. Suddenly, they are so beautiful to look at! It's like when you first fall in love with someone. Looking at their little finger, you think, "Oh gosh! It's so cute!" Or "look at that gorgeous nose!" It might be ten feet long, and yet, it is still beautiful to you (laughing). I know that when I'm aware of my Light and I'm aligned to Spirit, I really do see the beauty in everyone. There is nothing ugly in the Universe. Everything has got its own particular shape and form. Some people are more voluptuous than others, and some are really thin. However, it doesn't matter; it's beautiful, It's all beautiful.

Wilma: I was just going to say the very same thing about being aligned with Spirit. When you are aligned, you see beauty in all things because beauty is in all things. Each person is unique. In the multiplicity of everything, there is beauty running through it all. When I feel at peace, in harmony and joy, it is the time when I see the beauty in everything. Even when chaos is happening, we must pay close attention to be able to see through that mist, difficult as it might be. We must look through that chaos and know that beauty comes forth from within.

Michele: It's the appearance of chaos that causes us to think that there isn't beauty. There's beauty in a ghetto. There's beauty in the ocean. There's beauty everywhere. However, I think that it's a good idea to, while we are visualizing something, surround ourselves with beautiful things, even if it's something simple. I love the beautiful little teacup my Mum gave me last year. I'm appreciative of the good things in life because there is so much more good than there is bad. Even if you haven't traveled the world yet, there are magazines, books and videos from which you could appreciate the beauty of our planet. You can travel the world in front of your television set or your computer! You can view everything and visualize yourself being there. You might even feel the warmth of the sun on your skin, or other physical sensations. Everything starts in the mind; it's all in the thoughts. Take the word, beauty, for example. There are so many different ways of saying it. In Bahasa, Malaysia, it is "cantik," and in Italian, it is "bella." To quote the lyrics from one song: "Everything is beautiful in it's own way."

Wilma: There's a spiritual dance, originally from Persia, called "Sufi" dancing. It's a circular dance, and we move from partner to partner. There is an eye-to-eye connection, and we are able to see the beauty of God in each person as we pass from person to person. It's such a neat experience! It was quite challenging at first because there are some countenances you don't care for in the beginning; and you eventually get beyond that. Doing this type of dance is eye opening; it touches your soul, and it touches your heart. To be able to look into each person's eyes and see the beauty of God within them...now that is beauty!

Michele: Yes, I remember when I attended a seminar a many years ago, and we each had a partner. My partner was this lady; she must have been nearly six feet tall. She was big woman. Gosh, I'm only five feet tall and weigh about one hundred pounds. Now there we were, standing face-to-face. Our instructions were to hug each other, and I totally got caught in her chest. I'm thought to myself, "I don't like this hugging business." Then, we had to look at each other without speaking or touching. We were only about eight inches apart, looking into each other's eyes....I think it was for about five minutes. It was quite challenging for me to do that.

Some people giggled. I will certainly always remember her, for I'll always remember her eyes. I fell in love with her so to speak, or rather, I rose in love with her as a spiritual being. I became connected to her forever because we really got to see past the portals to each other's souls. I would recommend this to anyone, in any relationship. If this is a person that you know and especially if it is with your partner, just stop occasionally, and really look at each other, into each other's eyes. It brings you love. It's an amazing, eye-opening-to-the-soul experience. You see the beauty. You can see the beauty within as it's reflected back to you. If you feel uncomfortable with this experience, then you know that you really need to do it more often! Now, I love doing it. It's awesome! I love hugging now too. I know the beauty in everything is God, God in action... God everywhere.

Wilma: I can recall, many years ago Michele, gosh... it was probably back in the early 1950's, my father telling me the following story: He was working on a job. He was an electrical contractor, and there were some other men working with him. They were debating about who was the most beautiful woman in the world. Some chose Marilyn Monroe or some other starlets of that era. My father, when asked who the most beautiful woman in the world was, exclaimed "Eleanor Roosevelt." Now, Eleanor Roosevelt didn't have attractive looks, but she was one brilliant and beautiful woman on the inside. I remember him telling me that story. It has stayed with me for my entire life. It was so sweet to hear.

Michele: That is beautiful. He really must have been a wonderful man to see that in her. Too many times, we get caught up in what beautiful is "supposed" to be. Once upon a time, voluptuous, really big women were considered beautiful. Now the typical"beauty" is a finely muscled woman who works out all the time. Just a few years ago, it was really skinny twiggies. If we keep trying to be attracted to what we think is en vogue, then we'll never be happy. We've got to be content with who we are. I've got to learn how to do this too, because I love attractive looking people. However, it's always good to look beyond, see of what that person is made, and be aware of how this is reflected back to how we feel about ourselves.

Wilma: As I've progressed along on my spiritual path, I have found it much easier to see the beauty in all people....unless, of course, they are doing something to really annoy me (laughing)!

Michele: But what does that mean...?

Wilma: It means that I get to take a closer look at myself!

Michele: Maybe you just needed a day off (laughing)!

Wilma: Right! (also laughing) Life just gets more and more beautiful as I become more and more aware of all of these things that we have been talking about today. Each day is such a delight. It becomes easier and easier to see the beauty around us.

Michele: Life! Life! Life! The most beautiful thing in the world is living! The most wonderful gift that God has given us is LIFE. Equally important is the ability to think for ourselves, because if not, we would be like one of those beautiful plants, not knowing that we even had life. ?But I'll tell you what...those beautiful plants do know something! They know how to live in the moment. They don't worry about whether there will be rain today, or if the soil is rich enough for them to subsist.

Wilma: That is true (laughing). Yes, living in the moment is how to experience life. Look at the beauty of each moment, because really, that's all we have. Yesterday is gone, and tomorrow is always tomorrow. So all we really have is now. Just think on that a little bit. All we have is now. It goes from now, to now, to now, to now. It's great to plan and set your goals, as we have mentioned; however, it is not the goal that is important; it's the journey to the goal. When the goal is reached, there's always another goal and another goal... and you get goaled right out of life! Enjoy the beauty, the smells, the feeling, the emotion, the people, the energy...the God energy that is with you all the time. It's just so beautiful; it's not that I'm always present, but I do my best to be in the moment. I certainly forget sometimes and get caught up in the day's activities. This is where meditating is so powerful, because it brings me back to the present moment. It keeps me more in touch.

Michele: That is true. Just a simple deep breath helps me tremendously to live in the moment. Yes, I realize that before, I was an unconscious competent; I made things happen, but I wasn't consciously aware of how I was doing it. Now, I'm a conscious competent. I used to think about the past and then re-enact it. How many people say, "Oh, I always attract the same sort of partners," or, "You know they are always disloyal to me, etc." It is no surprise because THEY haven't changed, and they keep going back through the past. They continue to manifest the same events in their future through their thoughts. They are not creating new thoughts. It reminds me of that story about the person who walked to the city gate where he asked the guard, "What's this city like?" The guard questioned him in return, "Well, what was the city like from where you just came?" The man replied, "Oh, it was terrible. I had such bad luck there. I kept losing jobs and my wife left me... it was a horrible place. That is why I am searching for a happier place to live." The guard then told the man, "Dear traveler, this place is exactly the same. There are no jobs and there are unhappy people. I wouldn't come here." So, the man kept walking. Then another man came along, a couple hours later, and asked the same guard, "Dear sir, what's this city like?" The guard questioned him, "What was the city like from where you just came?" The traveler answered, "Oh, it was beautiful, positive, abundant...a beautiful city. I loved my life there and had great friends. However, I felt like visiting the world, even though I loved from where I came." "Well," said the guard, "This city is exactly the same; It's beautiful, positive, loving, and I know that we will love having you here. Welcome!" That is the truth about life! Some people study geography thinking they need to move to a new place in order to change their life...but unless we change who we are and live in the moment, right now, nothing changes. Above all, we have to recreate who we are, and the only way we can recreate our future is to recreate our nows. This is accomplished through our thinking. Live in the now, knowing that now is a totally new beginning. Only then can you stop negative karma from coming back to you. There is no need for that. There is only now.

Wilma: That reminds me of a little saying Michele, "Wherever you go, there you are." That is so simple and so true. I notice that people will change locations to feel better about themselves. They simply don't like where they are living. Sometimes, it helps for them to start off on a new footing. However, if they don't change their way of thinking, then they are going to drag everything with them again, packing it in their suitcase and taking it with them. Many times, it's more than just suitcases; it's vanloads! Know that you can start fresh right in the very moment. Leave everything behind and just start fresh. Change your thinking; do not drag the corpses from the past around with you. It was veryhelpful for me to become aware that I didn't have to go back and change anything in the past, but rather, be who I am today, and with the next step, right now, make that change.

Michele: By living in the now and even if the past does catch up to you, it has forever "changed!" My past is "different." All the people I knew are different. However, are they really different? No, I'm different. I'm the one who has changed. What happened? I get along so well with everybody now! I don't feel like people are criticizing me any more or judging me; I guess this means that I'm not judging them. And I don't have an attachment to it even if they are judging me. Wilma, do you know what I'm going to do? Because we are leaving today to go back home, I'm going to enter my apartment as if I've never lived there before, as if it's a brand new apartment and look at it anew. I'm already realizing that I need a few more plants and a little more brightening in my place. I'm going to go home, and I'm going to live in the moment! Even though I'm speaking about the future now, I'm teaching myself to live in the now. I'm not going to look at it as if it were yesterday. I have a brand new life with a brand new day. I love what Og Mandino said, "I greet this day with love in my heart. I live this day as if it was my last." Now that's living, that's life....... that is beautiful!!!

Wilma: When waking up in the morning, I say, "Today is a new day, a grand and glorious beautiful day...and I embrace it." Life....I really do love my life! Each day is so beautiful, grand and glorious. Even when things are presented to me in such a fashion that it appears to be challenging in the moment, I do know that it is all perfect and that whatever that is, it's come to teach me something. I look at the lesson. Each lesson is more and more beautiful. Life is beautiful!!!!

Michele: Wasn't that a great movie..."Life is Beautiful?" I think this is a wonderful time for us to simply acknowledge, in a beautiful prayer affirmation, the beauty of this moment...of this time within ourselves and watch it reflected and attracted back to us in all things in our life!...Nice chatting with you Wilma! You are beautiful!!!

Beauty

Dearest, dearest, Infinite....This day I feel You all around me. I see You in the beauty of this gorgeous, gorgeous planet called Earth...in this ocean of life, this beautiful ocean... calm, serene... and the beautiful rock formations. Also in the sands that were once rocks which over millions of years have turned into a beautiful beach, a place for us to lie down and enjoy yet another thing that You have created. I see You in the sun and in the beautiful palm trees...and in the grass and all of nature; You have created all of this, dearest God. I know You are creative and that You are the Creator. You are Infinite. You are The Infinite. You are everywhere present. You are all powerful. You are The Power. You are all knowledge. You are The Mind.. I breathe you in now. (Deep breath) You are all around me. You are in me....In my cells and in between the cells and You are flowing through me, just as the ocean is flowing. I do not need to think about which way to flow because I am flowing in the Right Divine way and the Right Divine time, always in all good, Divine Right ways. I AM the beauty of the ocean. I feel it within me. I AM the beauty of the sands of time. I know that the knowledge of all past, present and future is available to me but right now, all I am feeling is the beauty of this moment.

I AM beautiful. I am One with all beauty. This day is beautiful. Everywhere I look I see beauty on this day. Every pair of beautiful eyes I look into, I see beauty, I see life, I see The Infinite. I see beauty in the ghetto. I see beauty in the ocean. I see beauty on the streets. I see beauty in the desert. I see beauty in the marketplace. I see beauty in my home. Everywhere I look I see beauty. Thank you, God! Thank you God, for this day, for this moment, for this beautiful earth. I let go, knowing that this sense, this knowing-ness of beauty stays with me this day and

forever more. (Deep breath) I breathe it in now.

And so it is.

Notes

Beauty

Remember, if you do not have the answers to these questions,
take a nice deep breath and read through the chapter again.

1. What does it mean to be aligned with Spirit?

2. Why is it important to be content with who you are?

3. What is the most wonderful gift God has given us?

4. What is the best way to experience life?

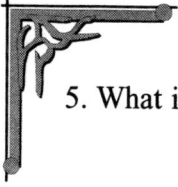

5. What is an unconscious competent?

6. What is a conscious competent?

7. When you want to change your life,

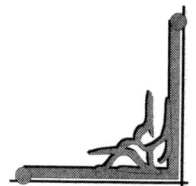

"Go thy way, and as thou hast believed, so be it done unto thee."

-Jesus Christ

Faith

Michele: Faith is a word that is misused often, like the word love. You know Wilma, some people say, "I believe!" To me, that's not really knowing; that's not really faith. "Oh, I believe that tomorrow the sun's going to shine." Well, of course! I've seen it happen every day... so yeah, the sun is going to shine. What would happen if I wasn't aware that there was going to be an eclipse tomorrow and then thought, "Oh gosh, my belief system is shattered now that the sun is not shining." I think of Faith as a knowing. When you know...that's called faith. You just know that the good is here. You totally expect it...just like we expect the sun to be up tomorrow morning. You don't just believe that the good is here, you know it is. That is the truth. That is the power behind it, and that is the Spirit. That is the wisdom of God, and this, to me, is faith. I have faith in life and in God or The Infinite Super Consciousness. Have faith in whatever you choose to call "God."

Wilma: Yes, you are right! It is not what we choose to call The Infinite; it is the feeling we get from the love we are receiving from God.

Michele: Now sweetie, that is Faith! I just love being your friend, you are such a beautiful soul Wilma! Faith, I know, is part of who I am....a powerful spirit having a physical experience. The unseen is the visible to me in everything I see. I know that once a flower was a seed; it is intended not to be viewed as a beautiful idea that God created, but rather, a flower that I now enjoy. I see in that flower a seed that was once an idea created by God. How could I not have faith? This ability has been built up over years of disciplining myself, affirming the truth, and meditating. Sometimes, however, it's not there; sometimes I don't feel like having faith. Do you know what the beautiful thing is? When I'm not feeling great and I begin to doubt, I am still aware that not even I have the power to stop my good. No one and no thing has the power over God. I know that even I can't stop my good because my faith is always there in the background.

Wilma: It's funny, I have a little different idea on faith. To me, faith comes before the knowing. It's having the Faith and the trust to hang in there. To me, you have to have the faith that it's going to work out, even before you know it will.

Michele: Well, I guess that's a paradox because if you have faith that it's going to work out, then you're knowing that it's going to work out. Eventually, when you witness more and more things working out, it gives you an even stronger faith...which is the knowingness. You have faith in the fact that you're going to breathe your next breath without thinking about it. That is faith!

Wilma: The faith is the glue that holds things together when you're on the journey of the unknown... because each day is an unknown. We have to step out there even though we don't know what's going to happen from one minute to the next. It's like going down a two-lane road with a line dividing it. You have faith that the car coming toward you is going to stay on the other side of the road. That is faith!

Michele: To me, it is much more. I believe that car is going to stay on the other side of the road. However, I do not know that it will, so therefore, I do not have faith that it will. Do you remember how you were saying that you don't really know what's going to happen, but yet,you do know that there is going to be good that occurs? Well, God is involved, no matter how the appearance. Here's a good one: How do you make God laugh? Tell him your plans (laughing)! I absolutely know that certain ideals I possess are going to come to fruition. What I don't know is how they are going to come to fruition. God knows how and when..."The Right Divine Time and the Right Divine Place." They are definitely going to happen. In my thoughts, I've already affirmed that they have happened. I just have to be an open channel with the knowledge that God knows how. I don't need to know how it's going to happen. I just have to be guided, take action, and do the work. That is my faith. My choice is to be wise and know that the "All Wise" knows how. The Spirit, the All Power, the All Knowing is running through me.

I am the vehicle, and I allow myself to be that vehicle. It reminds me of that beautiful song that Rev. Michael Beckwith and Ricki Byars wrote, "Use me, oh God, as you show me all that I must do." You see, I am the vehicle, and I stay on the right side of the road, unless of course, I am home in Australia where we drive on the left side of the road (laughing). I have faith in the knowledge that everything is going to be fine, no matter which way the road goes. Like I said before, my ending up in Malaysia wasn't part of my plan. However, it's helped to complete the Big Vision of my life without my realization at the time. God lets plans unfold as I let them unfold so that I can constantly have my dreams come to fruition. Now, I live in the USA. It's all part of God's wonderful plan for me!

Wilma: Having the faith that everything is going to turn out all right is such a beautiful feeling! You can just keep on keeping on and know that it's all going to turn out right, no matter what happens, no matter what the appearances are on the surface. As I saw more and more things for which I asked come into fruition, I acquired more faith in knowing that I was on the right track, that I was on the right path. Now I know that I am getting guidance; I can see that each day my faith becomes stronger and stronger.

Michele: And then you end up being in knowingness! You know, Vernon Howard, one of the great minds of our time, said, "I do not need to be strong. I just need to know that I am connected to that which is the strength." This is beautiful because I know that I don't have to be strong. I don't need to know how it's going to happen. I just know that God knows how. Wilma, I don't think religion has anything to do with faith. For me, religion is a teaching of a great philosopher or a great teacher, such as Jesus Christ, Ernest Holmes, Buddha, Vishnu, Mohammed, or another wonderfully awake individual. Whatever one's religious belief and practice, if it gets one through to true faith within themselves, then that's a wonderful accomplishment. One must not be doing it because the neighbors think one should go to church every Sunday. If one does it truly for one's own fulfillment, goodness me! Be the best you can be... as long as your religion is a result of your individual choice and not because of pressure from other people. If you're studying a particular so-called Faith because you want to do so and it feeds your soul... it can wake you up to LOVE! But I don't think that religion is Faith. I think faith lies within. However, if a particular religion brings you to that faith inside or that knowingness, then so be it. Good for you!

Wilma: There are times when we are overtly showing so much faith and strength in something that, to other people, it may appear absolutely ridiculous and simply wishful thinking. They may think we're nuts. However, at those times, we must just continue our faith, and keep on doing what we are doing. This is why it is best to refrain from telling others what you are doing unless they ask specifically. You retain more power that way. My minister, Dr. Rev. Harry Morgan Moses, made this statement, "The more spiritual you get, the higher you go," and then he will say, "Or the weirder you get." He means that you will seem weird to other people but you know that you're not weird.

Michele: Well, in Webster's Dictionary it defines "weird" as "having an extraordinary character." So, let's all be weird (giggling)! You know, Wilma, I do not know what "normal" is, and I don't really want to be normal if it means being part of the "status quo." Who knows what normal is? I have no idea, and I'm sure that, if my Dad was reading this book, he would definitely say, "That's my daughter, Michele...the weird and wondersome one." He used to say that. He wasn't being negative... it is just that I guess I have always gone out there and done my own thing. My Dad is actually very supportive of me and accepts me the way I am now. We have to step out, have faith and be an individual while doing what we know we must do and not what other people say they think we should do. Meanwhile, we have the knowledge that the wisdom is within us all, guiding us every step of the way. Wisdom doesn't equal intellect and it doesn't mean educational pursuits; it means allowing the Wise All-Knowing Father to guide us. Wisdom happens when we stop and listen and allow that power to flow through us. I find it best to ask God a question before I go to sleep. The answer nearly always comes the next morning, or, the morning after that. I just keep asking until I KNOW the answer and what it is I'm to do next. It's almost like, "click!"...the light has come on. Even though God is greater than we are, God is still within us. He's One with us and always there to guide us. That, to me, is practical "spirituality." That is Faith! We are looking at the most awesome, beautiful sunset right this second, thank you God!

Wilma: Wow, you are on a roll girl! And yes, this sunset is so beautiful! I know that it will rise tomorrow (smiling)!

Michele: I also believe that faith becomes stronger as we do more of something. We feel more confident about that pursuit, and it won't seem like a discipline anymore...it becomes a way of life....just like eating or breathing. That that faith is something that you know is inside of yourself. You don't have to be the one who can do it all; you don't have to be the strength. You can let go and let God. I know each and every one of us is absolutely equal in the eyes of God. All things are possible to all of us.

Wilma: I have faith in you girl! Just knowing that we are all One, that we are here in this experience to better ourselves and to grow, we are given a purpose, which, in turn, gives us joy. As each person discovers that, there will be more and more joy, and peace throughout the world.

Michele: All that we are focusing on now is peace within ourselves. We are not here to judge what happens. We can only start with ourselves.

Faith

My faith is a mental attitude, so I inwardly embody what my mind has always known. My Faith is complete and I now totally accept that I am always guided and looked after by The Infinite. I consciously generate Faith into every area of my beautiful, happy, healthy, abundant life. I know an invisible principle and law directly and specifically responds to my Faith.
My Faith has made me whole and complete.

Thank you Infinite! I let go and I let God.

And so it is.

Notes

Faith

1. Describe the meaning of faith.

2. How do you make God laugh?

3. Explain the meaning of Vernon Howard's quote.

4. What does it mean when we say that it's not important to know the how?

5. What does Wisdom mean?

"*Money is the servant; you are the Master*"

—Bob Proctor

MONEY

Michele: Money is such a wonderful gift because money is simply supply. Money is energy and an idea that allows us the freedom to live the way we choose to live. Money enables us to travel where we want to travel, to see that our dreams and visions come to fruition. I think that the biggest issue about money is the fear of money. People fight about money. One of the causes for war and bad relationships is money. The more we are in fear of it, the more we scare money away.

Wilma: Something that always confused me and what I could never understand was... how is money energy?

Michele: Money is energy; it is an idea. Money comes in all different forms. It's paper with ink printed on it. It's a credit card, and ultimately, it's an idea. It's simply an energy that allows us freedom, and if we think of it in that way, then we can then realize that we are the Master while money is the servant. In the past, people traded one thing for something else. They didn't always use so-called money. For example, a crop of corn may have been traded to enable you to shoe your horses. I believe that today, it is still good to view money this way, to see that we're just trading it to support our way of living. When we think of it this way, we can say that it's our supply and that it comes from the Infinite. I expect money to come from expected and unexpected channels, knowing that God is my source and supply, knowing that all channels are open. Money is all around me; it is there to support me in all my Right endeavors.

Wilma: It took me a long time to get my thinking there. It was one of the most difficult things for me. Eventually, I started to believe that money can come from anywhere. The usual way to think is, "Well, I have my job and I have my investments; that's from where the money is going to come. Where else can it come from?" I know that when I've kept an open mind, checks show up in the mail that I just never expected. Now, I have an open mind, and as I put forth my energy into my job, I know that money can and does come from any direction. I actually visualize this, placing myself in the center of a circle where I picture and feel money coming at me from all around. Pretty soon, something always shows up.

Michele: Money! What a hot topic! I believe that it is an even hotter topic than sex when it comes to people's reactions! Money is something we give and receive for services rendered in today's society. You know, Wilma, it's really important to charge for our services and feel good about it. There may be times when I will sing and I don't want to charge, so I just sing for the church or for whomever for free. It feels good to do this, however, it's also important that I receive something for my services and feel good about that too. People tend to be more appreciative of the service you provide if they have an investment in it. Someone has just handed over money for this book. The book appears to be comprised of only easy and natural conversations, but in fact, it has taken years of work on ourselves to get to the point where we feel good about sharing our life's experiences so that, in turn, you too can experience multi-dimensional abundance in your life! However, we still have to take action, i.e. to edit it and get it published, and so forth. I have faith that it will be done despite our having more work to accomplish. We grow in our awareness as we are taking action to get this book out there to people who desire to learn and grow. When I like a book that someone has suggested to me, I will often buy three or four copies. When I have read a book that has helped me to learn and grow, I immediately wish to share that it with others. It's good universal circulation.

Wilma: Yes, that was the word I was going to use, circulation. I was waiting for it to come; you have to let the Universe know that you are worthy. Some people hate using the word, "worthy," but I like using it!

Michele: I'm worthy! I'm worthy! I'm worthy (giggles)!

Wilma: If you don't let the Universe know that you are worthy to receive, then you're not going to receive. Or, if you do, then you might still find something for which to be ungrateful and that will stop your circulation of joy. So, we must state that we are worthy and accept all money for our services.

Michele: I think it's also important not to scare money away; money has ears, and it can hear you! That's why in "Be a Magnet to Money," the audio tape I did with Bob Proctor, we've got a song with these lyrics: "I am a magnet to money; I now have more than I need. I am a magnet to money, money, money loves me." You get the vibe that money is here to support you. It's your obedient servant. I often say aloud, "Money is my obedient servant." No matter what the appearances have been, and despite having faced a lot of challenges in my life, I always focus on the larger vision. I don't think about how the money is going to get here. I am resolved in making a decision, for example, this is the project I'm going to do, and it's going to be supported in every realm including the financial realm. And then, in the Right Divine place and the Right Divine time, it comes to fruition. Even now, I have projects on which I am working that require funding, and there are certain people who are beginning to lose faith in what I am doing. I do not need their faith. I know that God is in charge. I will keep taking action, with the knowledge that I will also be setting an example. However, I am doing it because I love to do it. I will never let other people affect my faith in what I am doing. Our dreams come to fruition if we just focus, do our affirmations and continue to surround ourselves with like-minded people who don't scare money away. And most importantly, we must never give up or allow ourselves to listen to those who have given up on us. I pretend to have burned my boat, now having only one choice-swim to new land and succeed. Some people will say, "Oh, there isn't enough money." Don't listen to those people; that is not the truth. There is an overabundance on this beautiful planet. However, what is most important is my attitude toward the different areas in my life. Know that keeping a positive attitude helps you manifest money in your life. It comes from unexpected sources in unexpected times.

Wilma: You never know when it's going to turn up...but, you just know it will! It's so important to give money because when you give, it opens up so much more room for that money to be circulated back to you. The more you give, the more that comes back to you, and many, many, times over. I've found that, in my real estate sales, sometimes I've had to give money to close a transaction for some reason, and I used to totally resent having to do that. I used to get so angry about it. Now, I know that when I give in that area, it will come back. Here's a very recent example: I sold property to a client and received a tiny commission. To make the deal work, I had to give up some of my commission; it barely left me anything. I was so struck by my client's joy that I made it work for her. Of course, the generosity was returned to me as I got another client who wanted to pay $1 million in cash for something. It just comes back to you over and over again...if you can willingly give and be happy and joyful about it This keeps the money circulation going. You are right. Money is energy. Money is the idea, and money is flow. We can remain in the constant flow of it.

Michele: I totally agree! I think it's wonderful and important to want to tithe, especially when giving to someone with whom you've been getting your spiritual strength. If you feel you don't want to give, then don't, because then, it's not going to come back to you. It's got to be in the joy of giving. There's a wonderful book which I recommend to everyone. It's called, "The Magnificent Obsession," by Lloyd C. Douglas. The book is about giving. Throughout the book, the main character says while he is giving money, "Do not tell anybody that I've given this to you"... and when people tried to give it back, he would say, "No you can't give it back to me. It's already been used up." So many people have had great success in their lives after reading that book. It was even made into a Hollywood movie. This is the way the Law of the Universe works: If you give, then you receive...and you always get back multiples of what you have given freely. We don't always immediately get back what we've given, but eventually, it will come back. Give because you want to give, not simply because you're expecting something back. Otherwise, it is just a trade-off, and that's not what giving is all about. It's about having the flow of a never ending cycle of increase and enjoyment. It's about being in the flow. When I first started reading about Louise Hay, she would talk about "blessing our bills." She also said that when the bills come in, you shall bless them. Someone trusted in us enough to turn on the phone service; someone trusted in us enough to give us a credit card. So, if they trusted in us enough, then we must trust in the Universe. Those bills will be paid on time. I think another good thing is to have open communication with your debtors, if you're in debt. It's important to be honest and let those people know, "This is where I am right now. I am going to pay you back, and I've got a plan of action to pay you back...starting now." Don't worry about whether they believe you or not. Just keep your faith. They will see that when you do pay them back, you were coming from integrity. Situations come up in life where we must keep our faith. It is so fulfilling, even though you're scared and you do owe bills, to communicate with the people to whom you owe money, so that they will feel confident in you. Then, you feel better and you avoid feeling fear. As soon as you are relieved of fear, the money will flow. I haven't always done this in the past because it was challenging to call people if I did not have the money right away. Just do it and call. Say, "Hey, I am here, and my intentions are good." That may not always make people feel at ease, and if they still are hard on you, do not become fearful, but rather, continue the Big Vision, while visualizing yourself paying them all back and seeing their happy faces.

Wilma: When I sit down and pay my bills, I joyfully pay the bills. Yes, you have to pay the "king." It's important to pay the "king," and what I mean by that, is, our taxes. Look at the beautiful country in which we live and all the good we have here. The country deserves money too. One ought not to get angry with the IRS or with the government because they are providing great services. When I pay my bills, I write on the back of my checks, at the very top where people will sign it, "blessings" to the tenth power...yes, even on the check to the IRS (giggling)! It's so much fun when you write that on the check.

Michele: Yes, that is wonderful! It proves how weird we both are... because I love doing that too. Do you know what else I think is important? I have learned a lot on this journey of life and in situations where I've been in debt and owed people money. They've called me and threatened me; they were so angry with me.... I would then allow myself to become fearful and to become angry and resentful with them as well. It was ridiculous. I wasn't letting the money flow. Now, if anything ever happens like this, it's so wonderful because I just say, "Look, this is absolutely going to get paid-trust me, believe in me." And then I pay it as soon as I am able. After it's paid, everybody is blessed. Even as the threats were happening and the apparent disappearance of moneyflow, I kept visualizing it come into my life. I stayed the course. And so, it started coming back into my life and I started paying people back at the level of what I could afford at the time. Hence, they would then know that I was coming from integrity and trust. The one thing I remembered during the time when people didn't believe in me, when they thought I had forgotten about them, was that I knew that I was going to pay them back. And I never, not even for a second, doubted myself. It didn't matter what they thought of me and said about me. After you've paid them back, goodness me, it's so funny when these same people call up and say, "I always believed in you." They must be true, otherwise they would have never allowed me to be in their energy to begin with. I learned a lot of lessons about being really honest about when you think you can pay somebody back. If you really don't know, then say, "Look, this might look risky; but this is what it is, and I have every intention of paying you back. And this is the way I'm going to do it." So, if this has happened to you in your life, then forgive yourself and move on, knowing that it is all going to happen right...at the perfect Right place and at the perfect Right time. "Never give up! Never, never give up!" the wonderful Winston Churchill once said.

Wilma: It is also very important to be open to receiving. To be open to receiving the good is so important. People have to learn how to receive because it completes the cycle of the giving, the good, and the money coming to you. I always enjoyed giving, but I had the hardest time receiving. Sometimes, it's really difficult to graciously receive without having to give back to that person. To be able to receive is hard for people that are real giving people. When that circuit is open, more and more will come to you.

Michele: It's all about consciousness. The more we stay focused and are with like-minded people, the more comes into our existence. The "The Science of Mind" course, developed by Ernest Holmes, taught me so much! So did "Unity" and many other teachings that I now love. To me, Jesus Christ was the greatest teacher of all. The following quotes are timeless: "These things that ye see me do, ye shall also do... and greater." "It is YOUR faith that made you whole." Taking classes and going to seminars are wonderful ways of learning. There, we get to meet others who want to improve their lives. It's all about consciousness, recognizing the power that is there, that is now available, and unifying with it. However, you may not live in an area of the world where there are such classes available. Then, perhaps you could look at home study courses on the internet, etc. There are also books and audio programs authored by many great teachers. There are, for example, Jack Canfield, Mark Victor Hanson, Bob Proctor, Brian Tracy, Ernest Holmes, Allan Parker, Ralph Waldo Emerson, Rev. Christian Sorrenson, Dr. Rev. Harry Morgan Moses, Thomas Troward, D. Michael Rideout, Asara LoveJoy, Annella Faye, Louise Hay, Chris Michaels, Wendy Keller, Stuart Wilde, Gene Mitchener, Earl Nightingale, Napoleon Hill, Norman Vincent Peale and so many others! I am naming all of these authors because I highly recommend all of their works. Just taking a simple accounting course for yourself, so you can learn how to balance your own checkbook, is self-actualizing. It's not only metaphysics we can learn. Let's consider anything that can empower and educate us. Let's go beyond wishful thinking and into real manifestation. I'm learning things now about business that I thought I would never learn and that I thought were too challenging. However, I went ahead and studied them anyway. It empowers us to learn, because then we are using the greatest faculty that God gave us...the power of THOUGHT!

Wilma: It's not just the expecting; it's the accepting. Many times, we could expect something negative to happen and for some reason, some kind of fear develops. I don't believe that I'm good enough to achieve something sometimes, but despite this feeling, I tend to expect positive outcomes anyway." Totally embrace it and expect it as yours! Claim it! All of the good in the universe is yours to have! There's no such thing as too big; there's no such thing as too little! God doesn't know big or little. It CAN be yours!

Michele: And it's nothing to do with "luck" either. Some say, "Oh, that person was born under a lucky star." No! We are all exactly where we need to be, right where we are now. Do not wait until you have the money and think that then you'll be happy; it will never happen. We must learn to be happy right now, with what we have right now. Oprah Winfrey said that, if she hadn't been happy to begin with, she probably would not have had such great success. Look at all the good she is doing now with the money she has created. It is important to be happy right now, where we stand. She's created these wonderful T.V. shows; she helps people get their wonderful books out to the public, and she is a living example of "walking her talk." She started with nothing but an idea and a desire to do more with her life. There are so many different things to do! It doesn't matter where you were born. If you were born into wealth or born into poverty, whatever education you received or whatever talents you feel you have or don't have, you can create whatever you want. There are so many abundant people who have little education. It's not that I don't think education is wonderful; I think all types of education are wonderful. And, it has nothing to do with luck. It is our attitude that counts. Somebody once said to me, that luck means "laboring under correct knowledge." Who wants to labor? No, thank you! To me, luck stands for "learning under correct knowledge," or perhaps, "loving under correct knowledge." This is the Universal Law. It is the Law of the Universe that money is here for all of us. If every single person on this planet had a share of all of the money on the planet right now, then everyone would be millionaires. It is all about having a "prosperity collective consciousness." I believe that the money, after a while, would end up back in the hands of that small percentage of individual who originally had it.

Wilma: The more abundant people that are out there, the more abundance is created. There is absolutely no limit. The creative Power of the Universe is only for fuller expansion. Forever expanding upon itself....that is the way it is. The more people who have abundance, the more abundance will happen to people. The more you surround yourself with beautiful things...the more beautiful things are attracted to you. When I'm surrounded by beauty, I know that I'm in the "expansive" mode and that more and more is coming back to me. So, I surround myself by beauty and like-minded people all the time.

Michele: You do! When I walk into your place Wilma, it's serene, in divine order, and beautiful. I just love your place; it is truly beautiful! Also, it is important for us to remember to keep things in divine order. If you don't, right this second, have the money to run right out and get that beautiful sofa, or whatever it is you want, well then visualize it. Cut it out of a magazine and say, "I now give thanks that I have this beautiful sofa"....and it WILL come to you. It's also important to remember to keep a clean place where you live. My mother once bought me a beautiful tea cup. When I'm at my computer, I love to sit there with my nice pot of Earl Grey tea and drink from my beautiful tea cup. Bring down all your good silverware and nice stuff now; don't just keep it for the guests. Be your own guest!

Wilma: There is one saying that I love, and I almost forgot to tell you. "Grow where you are planted." Start right where you are and start expand from right where you are, bit by bit. Sometimes, it's really hard for one to do this, to stretch their thinking. I suggest starting with a little bit and seeing what you can do to improve your situation right now.

Michele: It's important to remember about multiple sources of income. Bob Proctor talks about this powerful tool in our, " Be a Magnet to Money," audio program. If you haven't listened to the program, a multiple source of income is income that comes to you while you are off doing something else. A "PSI," or Permanent Source of Income, is income you earn while on-site working. An example of a multiple source of income is when you're in a network marketing company where you get your royalties, or product earnings, while you are sleeping. Network marketing companies are great for people who aren't yet sure about what they want to be doing. Building income via a company that has a great product and which helps people is a good thing. As a songwriter and author, I receive royalties. Even though I could be sleeping, someone may be playing my song on a radio in another country, and subsequently, I would receive a royalty check. This is a multiple source of income, but when I'm on stage singing, this is considered a permanent source of income because I have to be present to earn the money. So, it's important that you have two ways of making money. There are people at work and money at work. I'm not a certified investment advisor, but I'm giving you good examples of multiple sources of income and a few different things that you can do. Just know that you are a magnet to money!

Money

Money is my obedient servant.
I love people and use money.
I do good with my money
knowing it is in a never ending
cycle of increase and enjoyment.

I am a magnet to money.
I now have more than I need.
I am a magnet to money.
Money, money loves me.

Money, money loves ....
(sign your name)

Notes

Money

Remember if you do not have the answers to these questions,
take a nice deep breath and read through the chapter again.

1. Explain the meaning of the quote: "money is the servant.
You ar
the master."

2. What are the biggest issues people have about money?

3. Explain how "money is energy."

4. Explain how "God is my source and supply."

5. Why is it fun to give money and to tithe?

6. Who do you tithe to?

7. Why is it important to receive?

8. Name some ideas for multiple sources of income for you. Act on them now! Remember, all things are possible, so think BIG!

"Love is Everything."

LOVE

Michele: Wilma, you know I love the love word. After all, love is everything......I don't know if I ever told you that one of my bands in Australia was actually called L.O.V.E. which stood for, "Love Of Vast Experience." I think that's what love is all about. It is about enjoying every experience and having that feeling of peace, joy and fulfillment. Our friendship means so much to me and the love that I feel for you, it's almost as if you are God manifest in human form. I feel that and see that within you. When we do our prayers together, the love that I feel from the unification of spirit is so beautiful.

Wilma: I feel that too, and I don't even know how to describe it (laughing)! It's beyond description! You have to experience it. There are absolutely no words for love. There was a special time, a time when I was meditating, and then, all of a sudden, I had this powerful, incredible love experience. That's the only way to describe what it was. This light came through me, and it was so powerful. I had to lie on the floor, take all my clothes off and have the experience; it was so profound....

Michele: I remember you telling me that (laughing)!

Wilma: And there I was, feeling like I was glowing from everywhere and all this love was just flowing through me. I stayed that way, with this love, for over two hours. It was the most incredible experience.

Michele: Did it feel sensual? What was it?

Wilma: Well, actually all of it. It started off as love coming through me, and then it became a sensual feeling. It was different kinds of love feelings coming together all at once...and it was a love for everything around me. I had so much flowing through me that I had to think of people to whom I had to send my love (Wilma laughing).

Michele: It is so beautiful because it's unification with spirit. Actually, it is normal and natural for us to feel this, and it is the reason why some people get so scared of love...because it is so intense sometimes when our energy rises in love to that level. I feel that it may also be the reason why so many of us do our very best to block that feeling when it comes into us at such high levels; they may try to drink it away, or watch copious amounts of TV, or whatever. When we're not feeling that sort of love, it keeps us in a comfort zone of flatness.

Wilma: Good point!

Michele: But you know what happened to me once, Wilma? I had a crush on this guy, and I found out that it was unrequited love, that he didn't feel the same way towards me. But then, all of a sudden, I had this experience that was so different for me; all of a sudden, I felt the amazing honor of being given the gift of being able to love another. So, rather than having my ego wallow in self-pity and pain, I felt great to be given the honor of loving someone. I realized then what "unconditional love" is. It is where we can really love someone by not needing him or her to love us back. Because of this attitude, I was insulated from hurt and disappointment.

Wilma: It is beautiful to be able to be so certain of the love that's coming through you, from the Universe and the Creative Power of the Universe. It's great to know that you can send it back and realize that you are benefiting them while they aren't even aware of it (both laughing).

Michele: Yes, that is very cool indeed.

Wilma: (Wilma laughs) It is so nice to be able to experience love. Sometimes, when I see a homeless person walking along the street, I feel the light and the of love of God flowing through me and then out towards that homeless person. I'm sure there's nobody out there to love them, and they're perhaps not in touch with the love that

God has for them. Just by extending my heart and doing things for people about whom I don't even know anything, I receive such a beautiful feeling.

Michele: That reminds me of something said by Stuart Wilde. I love Stuart Wilde's teachings throughout his books and tapes. He said, "Do not feel sorry for people as how do we know who those people really are. They could be some great walking sage that just sent us the love that we just felt back to them." It's so interesting how we never really know, so therefore, it's good to be in the moment of love, for all. Do you know what is an awesome experience? It is to express that love for someone in a personal sexual relationship; It is a wonderful and magical feeling. When you feel that love for yourself and your universe, then you are whole, and you end up attracting to yourself another whole person rather than your "better half." You are two whole people together in love with each other's soul.

Wilma: Oh, I totally agree with that! Because if you're sure about who you are and in love with yourself, then all the aspects of you have blossomed. There have been times when we may feel a longing and neediness, and so that is what we end up attracting.... a whole lot of neediness and co-dependence. But, if you are looking at it from the standpoint of giving and being, then it all comes back to you as whole, complete and perfect. To be able to be unified with yourself and also with the other person, and yet, still be individuals who do your own things and allow the other person to be their own separate person...it is such a healthy and great way to experience love in relationships! Then, if needed, we can release the other person if that is required to allow them to be themselves...instead of sucking out their life force by staying in the relationship (Wilma laughs).

Michele: Sounds like you have experienced the "sucking type" my dear (Laughing)!

Wilma: Oh yes, I thank God that experience is long gone.

Michele: It's really funny; a friend of mine was talking to me about how he really loved me. He was telling me all the reasons why I had these hang ups and why I wouldn't love him back. I just wasn't attracted to him in that way, but I did have affection for him ...just not how he wanted it. So many people ask, "What do you mean you love me, but you aren't in love with me?" Well, there are so many different ways of loving. When you feel passion towards someone, you rise in love with them. You don't fall in love, you rise in love. It's experiencing Divine emotion as being in synergy together.

Wilma: Oh yes! There's a synergistic effect when the energy compiles; compounds and expands; it creates even more and more love. We attract others to us who are in that same vibration of love.

Michele: It is all God, and God is LOVE!

Wilma: There is more love in the world than anyone can fathom. If we can embody a little bit of that love and then expand it so that it comes back to us even more greatly expanded....

Michele: This is why I wrote the affirmation song, "I AM LOVE," because it is a love song to ourselves, about ourselves. We MUST know that it all begins in acknowledging this truth.... I AM LOVE.

Wilma: Yes! This is so hard to remember sometimes. As soon as we get up in the morning, let's all put a banner in front of our bed (Wilma laughs) that reads, "I am love"...in order to affirm it daily.

Michele: Yes! Because if we continuously reprogram our minds with this idea, we become that idea and emotionalize it. Everybody is love, pure love. I like to walk around and say, "Everywhere I look, I see the eyes of God." If I'm not feeling aligned, this affirmation helps me get back on track and away from self-absorption. I simply and silently say to myself, "Every pair of eyes I see, I see the eyes of love."

Wilma: Oh, that is beautiful!

Michele: As John Lennon said, "All we need is love!" So, let's affirm now that we are LOVE!!!

I am LOVE

I'm in touch with who I am,
I am love woman and man.
I'm in touch with who I am,
I am Love.

I'm in touch with who I am,
Mother Nature is my land.
I'm in touch with who I am,
I am Love

I am love.
Yes, I experience the power of love,
Because I am love...
Oh yes, I am love!

I believe my soul to be,
Living in God's endless dream.
I believe my soul believes,
It is love.

Love heals me with love's gentle touch,
Unconditionally with loving trust.
Warm and tender,
Yes, I know...
I am love!

Notes

Love

1. Explain why love is everything.

2. Meditate for a few minutes on love:
Sit quietly..Breathe in and feel the light of love above you. Inhale
that light of love through you and your entire being. Let the love
flow in and then let it flow out with each breath. Affirm to yourself "I AM LOVE." Whenever you feel out of balance, stop and
give yourself a love tune-up. Love is the decision, so decide on
LOVE.

3. Why is it important to love yourself first?

4. What is a healthy way to experience love in relationships?

5. Practice looking in people's eyes and say quietly to yourself, "here in these eyes I see love..." no matter how each person appears to you physically or emotionally. Just do it! Miracles will happen for you as you begin to feel love.

"If I hold you with my emotions
you'll become a wished
for
companion.
If I hold you with my eyes,
you'll grow old and die.
So I hold you where we both
mix with the Infinite"

-RUMI

Relationships

Michele: Wow, another great topic for conversation..... relationships! There are so many types of relationships that we experience in our life, from finding out what a real friend is, to lovers, to children, to our siblings and our parents. There are so many different types of relationships, but it all begins with me. It makes no difference how anyone else's personality is within a relationship because it ALL has to do with how I respond. I am totally responsible for how every relationship in my life turns out. In all my relationships, I am mirroring back to myself how I feel about myself. So, if I wasn't getting along with my sister, for example, I'd be mirroring back how I was really feeling about myself. I now have a great relationship with my sister, and I see all the good in her. I no longer act defensive, and I am aware of her wonderful sense of humor and all the great stuff about her. She is a generous, loving, caring person.. This has happened because I have forgiven the past, forgiven myself and finally grown up. I am seeing the good in myself now; it's being reflected back, and it's such a beautiful thing for me. I now take total responsibility... a topic which we've talked about so many times, Wilma.

Wilma: We sure have discussed that topic, oh yes!

Michele: I still clearly remember the day when you told me how, when I was in that unusual relationship with a particularly hard-to-communicate-with man, I was simply mirroring back to myself the deep feelings and things I had not resolved in other relationships. Now, I can see how that also included the relationship with my sister. I was defensive with this man, as I had been with my sister, and I allowed myself to feel that I had to prove myself to him. Even though I did not like to hear this at the time, boy, was that the truth! However, if we can truly see that we are not being acknowledged in a relationship and we've really asked them to communicate but they will not, then I think that we have to step back and see whether or not this relationship is for our highest good. Sometimes, it's important to know when to leave a relationship because its not healthy.

Wilma: Oh yes, Michele! I totally agree. Those relationships are in our lives for a reason...so that we may grow. We can't be living in a cave somewhere, because then, you don't grow. Each person that has come into my life, whether I perceived them at the time to be a minus or a plus, was actually a plus, now that I look back on it. It was all a positive! They were "gifts" that I had attracted and I could finally SEE when I "woke up". Today, when things do pop up, I am much more AWARE. When somebody says something that bothers me, I know that this is something in my life that needs to be healed. If one can look at everything in that way, when something hurtful is said, take a moment to pause, step back, look at it, and say, "Well, that is inside of me and needs to be healed." I find that this attitude really makes all of my relationships a lot easier and fulfilling. Now, there are times when, as you said, Michele, that it's no good to have a particular relationship in your life anymore... because it's already served its purpose for you. Sometimes, it's just time to move on! These are things about which to pay close attention. There are people in my life with whom I've been friends since I was a little kid. They're still close friends despite having others who come into my life briefly... but its all been good. It is illuminating for us to look back on these close relationships to see how we have grown from each experience...whether it was with friends, parents, siblings, a spouse or lover.

Michele: Yes, oh yes! It's also about communication. Sometimes, we do require the art of diplomacy so that we don't hurt people. It is all about clear and grounded communication. I do not believe though, that we can really "hurt somebody's feelings." For example, if we think we are hurt, then we can ask ourselves, "Why do I feet hurt?" Asking ourselves questions in this way is a very powerful exercise in taking responsibility for our own feelings. As you know Wilma, I met this wonderful male friend, and I discovered that my feelings for him were starting to grow deeper than just friendship, and lets face it, I had developed a good old fashioned crush. We had been talking a lot, and I thought that maybe it was time for me to move out of my celibacy, as he is such a great person with a wonderful caring and spiritual personality. Anyway, it ended up that he only liked me as a friend; and at first, I was a bit sorry for myself, until I realized what a blessing he was in my life as a friend. It's wonderful that I have established a great relationship with this wonderful person with whom I can connect and communicate so well. I didn't want to sever that just because the relationship wasn't the way I thought it was supposed to turn out. Once I got out of my ego and really looked at him and myself, even though we got along so well as friends, I realized that what he desired in a loving relationship was very different from how I live my life. Our lifestyles would have clashed eventually. God always works in wondrous and perfect ways.

Wilma: There are lots of times when we don't know what's for our highest good. However, you are right...God always knows (chuckling). Someone or something will come into our lives that seems to be quite painful to us, and it happens at the time when we think that it is not for our highest good. But perhaps it is! Being aware of this is very powerful!!!

Michele: Another area in relationships about which we can discuss, is another's behavior. Let's say that there's a person in my life, and they are doing something that is not acceptable to me....well then, I do not have to be involved in any way whatsoever. I have to follow my own path and do it without judging others. I must simply allow myself to know what is or is not acceptable behavior when I am with them. Now that could be anything. I have a friend who enjoys nude sunbathing at a nude beach; that's not acceptable to me or even something I would enjoy doing, but I don't judge them. I just don't choose to go to the nude beach with them, but we are still friends. Sometimes, my friend invites me to go to body painting parties. I just don't go to those parties at which I would feel uncomfortable. It's not that they are wrong; it's just that it's not right for me. If there are a ton of behaviors in which we find our friends engaged, that are truly unacceptable to us, then it is probably time to reevaluate that relationship...and maybe move on.... NEXT (laughing)!

Wilma: Yes, it is good to say to yourself, "Okay self, my lesson has been learned with this person; I have grown, and now I am leaving!!!" And then we are out of there!

Michele: You said it (Laughing)! Particularly if you are in a relationship with someone and they say to you, "But honey, it's really good for our consciousness for me to be out with other women because you know, that's freedom." That's a definite, NOT ACCEPTABLE and NEXT!!!

Wilma: When we recognize when to say "Next," it becomes essential to our happiness and success in all areas of our lives. Relationships do affect all areas of one's life, as you mentioned before.

Michele: Exactly! We may not always see it at first, but they really do. This is great news because, when we are in a supportive, like-minded relationship, it helps to create good in all the other areas of our lives. Our friendship has certainly been a very positive and supportive experience in my life...for which I always thank God! I love ya Wilma!!!

Wilma: Thank you, honey. You know there are times when you can get so caught up in stuff that you can't see it. You have to pull yourself away and take a long look at it, otherwise, or somebody else WILL wake you up!

Michele: Oh yes, ain't that the truth! When we are communicating with someone (and we must communicate to be in a successful relationship) well, if there are too many things that trigger us and with which we just do not agree, then we must find out whether it is within us, or, it's just unacceptable behavior. As I mentioned before, as long as we do not get into judging others, the only thing to do is to step away from that energy and give yourself time to meditate into that silent, special place in order to find out what is really going on. As Deepak Chopra says, "Get to that place between the spaces. The Gap...wherein lies all of our answers." Now that is important. If a relationship is important to us, we really HAVE to make a decision to put time into it and to love that person unconditionally. When it gets to the point where you can openly communicate with that person, tell them, "We need to communicate. Please open up, just tell me what you really think." Recently, I said this to someone who was shy, and they found it hard to communicate. Shyness is really a lack of confidence and self-esteem; shyness shows that we are still worrying about what other people think. Now getting back to the point...I said to my shy friend, "Well, if you cannot speak to me in person, then write it in a letter and send it to me...just get out what it is that you are feeling." That is easier for some people because then, they're in their own space. This is helpful if either party feels that the live communication taking place in each other's presence will end in anger. That's why I love e-mail (laughs)! E-mail is very cool. You can just e-mail it back! If someone has emailed me something about which I disagree, I will, at that time, see if there is negative emotion involved. If so, I might not read it straight away, but rather, stop, and perhaps wait until the next day. Only then will I send them back a reply after careful and honest reflection.

Wilma: In my last relationship, the guy would send me faxes. That actually worked out just as well.   Later, he would send me letters; this was after our relationship ended. The letters showed a lot of his pain, blame and judgment, and yet, I was able to set it down. If he had told me, in person, everything that he had written, I probably would have lost it right then and gone into a major defensive mode. But then, it was really neat because I responded back in loving-kindness. After I responded back in loving-kindness, it turned him around for a little bit. It is so healthy to get that out of your system, be able to respond, in kindness, and let the person go.

Michele: That is so great sweetie! I love that you are so grounded in your belief and faith, and you totally walk your talk!

In fact, you also talk your walk (laughs)! It's all about communication. Sometimes, people, for whatever reason, feel that they are co-dependent upon you. They may not even realize what is going on. They want to continue to have a relationship with you and can say lots of manipulating things, particularly when they are new to metaphysics. Sometimes they feel that they are all knowledgeable and know what is best for the whole world. I was exactly the same. We have lessons yet to learn, but we can learn those lessons away from that kind of person. If you're not feeling your joy with them, then to me, its pretty simple. Generally, if the greater percentage of time with that person is spent feeling great and happy, then that speaks for itself. If you feel good about yourself when you are with that person, then it's clear as a bell. That is a good, healthy relationship. It's not about what they need from you. It's not about what you need from them. It's simply about the enjoyment you feel being in that relationship. If it is fulfilling, and you feel good about yourself, then THAT is what I call a good relationship. When we are constantly in a down vibe with another person and feel immediately relieved and wonderful when they are gone, well HELLO! Wake up and smell the roses!!!

Wilma: Also Michele, in relationships, those that are healthy are mutually beneficial. There are many things that make up a good relationship, and being like-minded is a key ingredient. I do not imply enjoying the same hobbies; I am talking about being on the same spiritual level. Two halves don't make a whole; but it's important to be in a synergistic relationship where each of you empowers the other...and then builds on that foundation. To me, that is the perfect relationship.

Michele: That, my dearest friend, is how we decided to do this book (smiling)! We had many great conversations, and we continue to do so now. It's such a wonderful thing! We do not live in a cave, all alone. To be happy and fulfilled in life, we have to forget about being, "The Lone Ranger!" Ask yourself this question when you became involved in a sexual relationship: "If I wasn't having sex with this person, and I was just there to hang out with them and be friends, would I still choose to be with them?" That is a very good question! If the answer is an absolute "Yes!" because you love them as a friend, and because they are so much fun, and you feel good when you are with them, then both of you deserve a big CONGRATUATIONS! But if you can't find more than five things that you like about them, then ooh honey, maybe there's a "NEXT" there too....

Wilma: That is such great advice! I love that Michele! I see that you have been learning from your past. That's good to hear (giggles). Lust can really blind you sometimes. But then, as that wears off, the newness of the passion dies off and you start to see these bonds crumbling before you. Perhaps that was what was needed for your growth!

Michele: You believe it's what you need at the time because perhaps there is something within you that is not feeling fulfilled. It's never about sex. When we have sex for this reason, it's something else that we need to have fulfilled and to experience. Relationships is a topic about which we could talk for a long time! However, let's start an affirmation about attracting wonderful, like-minded friends and about keeping our relationships wonderful, fulfilling and supportive...because that's who we are. That's who we choose to be ourselves...supportive, wonderful, loving friends to one another. Think about what we want to attract in our lives and in our relationships, and learn to be that way. Be a good sister, a good daughter, a good mother, a good friend, a good lover, a good listener; there are so many things to become, and yet, it's SO hard when we are in our humanness to be the best we can be, but at least we can strive towards it.

Relationship

All of my relationships are perfect,
because trust begins with me.
All of my relationships are perfect,
because love is always free.

I now attract wonderful, like-minded friends.
My relationships are loving, healthy, beautiful,
honest, fulfilling and supportive.

My relationships are based on
respect, love and understanding,
That's who I choose to be
a supportive, wonderful friend
to all the people in my life.

All of my relationships are perfect
because trust begins with me.
All of my relationships are perfect
because love is always free.

Notes

Relationships

1. What does the statement "all relationships begin with me mean?"

2. Write down several ways you have grown from a relationship experience.

3. Take responsibility for your feelings and ask why you felt hurt in any past or present relationship. Don't blame the other person. Write down all these feelings.

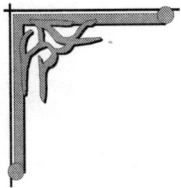

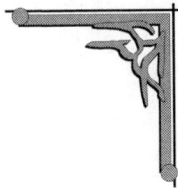

4. Where do all of our answers lie?

5. What is the meaning of shyness?

6. Name several ways you can improve your relationships by taking responsibility.

7. Is there a relationship that may need to be released from your experience because it is no longer serving you in a positive way? If so, release it with love, forgiveness and responsibility.

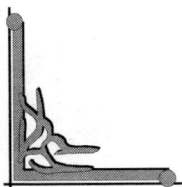

"Intuition is God in man revealing to him the Realities of Being"

-Ernest Holmes

Intuition

Michele: Intuition to me is simply The Infinite speaking to me. I am in tune with God. I know that all the knowledge and creative ideas that have ever existed, are, or will be, totally available to me when I stop and listen. Ernest Holmes, the great metaphysician who wrote, "The Science Of Mind" said, "Intuition is not a strong emotion because when we feel emotional, it is usually our old thinking." It is our old paradigm reacting to a situation in our human experience. Intuition is that still, small, quiet voice. It's just that knowingness. It's the mystic. A "mystical" experience is God speaking through us. A psychic experience is all of the different thoughts that are in the Collective Unconscious. People become confused between the two. Intuition is the Infinite directly speaking to us; it is a wonderful and magical power that we can all tap into when we stop and listen.

Wilma: That is wonderful... and yes, Ernest Holmes was a very awake soul! Intuition shows up in many different ways. I believe that, at different times, we all experience it in different ways. Some people will hear a voice, and some people get a "feeling." Or, some people will get a vision. With me, it's kind of a combination of these things. I have had voices come to me, and I've also had feelings. I have had a voice just tell me.

Michele: What do you mean by "voices?" Do you actually hear a voice like we are speaking now?

Wilma: I can hear a voice like my own voice, with the exception that when it says something, I have to act on it immediately... because I know that it can literally save my life. It comes to me as a very, deep voice or command: "You must do this or that."

Michele: That's great Wilma, because this is what we all need...guidance from the Infinite. You've experienced a true knowing, and this is how it comes to you, through your sub-conscious. That's awesome!

Wilma: And then, there are other times when there's a lighter voice that will tell me to become a minister. At first I said, "No way and WHY?" But then I had a conversation with that voice, and I asked it to, "Show me!"

Michele: I want to talk about this more Wilma, please continue....

Wilma: The voice quietly said, "Look at the poster on the wall." And so I read it. I forgot exactly what it said, but it said something about following through on something. I discounted it, and said, "Naaaa....That's not good enough! Show me something better or clear. So, as I walked to the back of the room and toward the minister of my church, just then, his mother-in-law came up to me and said, "You know, you'd make a great Minister!"

Michele: Oh wow! That is wonderful when it comes that clearly! The message comes through people, or from someone on the television or radio; they will say the exact same thing that we had asked about previously or perhaps where to go.

Wilma: By being aware and paying attention, it allows for our intuition to become very clear. Meditation puts us more in touch with the Infinite because intuition is, in fact, the Infinite guiding us every step of the way. As I become more spiritually savvy, I am much more aware of the role intuition plays and look for its guidance. It is now so clear.

Michele: Yes! It's so wonderful when we are clear. If you remember, I was in a business situation a few years back, where I met some business people, and the business deal they offered me seemed so logically wonderful. It looked GREAT! But, deep within me, that small nagging voice kept saying, "no" to doing business with these people. It just didn't feel right. I didn't feel synergy with the situation or with those people. They were saying all the right things; however, it did not feel right. It felt like such a difficult decision at the time as I really could have used the funding that this opportunity seemed to have promised for my business. As it turned out, it was not, in fact, the best business decision, because I chose logic over intuition. Now, I hope that I have learned that, no matter what, I must follow my Intuition. Boy, that was a heavy lesson! It took me a long time to get over it. However, with God's help, I did it! It's really simple! We can be guided into right actions, whether it be in personal relationships or in making business decisions. There are over six billion people on our wonderful planet with whom to be in business, and if something doesn't feel quite right and it doesn't feel in the flow, then your intuition is telling you that there is something, or someone, far more suitable for you to be connected with and to enjoy being with. I feel it's very important to let it go and trust. God knows what our path is...spiritual growth and happiness. It is important to listen to that small voice and then follow what we know is right to do. Doing what makes us happy means following our intuition. When we are feeling happy and when things are flowing with ease and grace, we know that we are on the right path.

Wilma: This is joy! It's so incredible! It feels like you are floating along your path; it just feels so right. I've learned to talk to my intuition, asking it for guidance for even simple things... like finding a parking space!

Michele: It's funny you should mention a parking space....Maybe we need to find a parking space a few blocks away from here... because we need the exercise (laughing)! I heard Terry Cole Whittaker say this, and it just cracked me up. That certainly gets us out of judging everything and lets us know that all is exactly the way it is meant to be.

Wilma: Sometimes, if I'm looking for an address while driving, I'll ask, "Okay, which way? Turn right?...Turn left?" (giggle) It's so much fun when you are playing with that, just to see what fun experiences can and do show up.

Michele: I would like to reiterate on the idea that it important to get emotion out of the way. Just be quiet and listen...because it is a powerful thing. Everyone is intuitive. People say, "Oh, that person is really psychic." Well, everybody is psychic! We've all got a "sixth sense." We all pick up on the energies that are happening beyond the physical. A very simple, sometimes surprising and yet common example is when the phone rings and the person on the other end is someone you were just about to call. This happens because we do connect with people beyond our normal consciousness, and our intuition leads us to whatever is for our highest good. I now know to never be afraid of what life at the moment is looking like, just as I know Spirit is leading us all. All we have to do is stop and listen. This has taken me to places like Malaysia with Bob Proctor and enabled me to work with many wonderful, like-minded people. I ended up working in Australia with Deepak Chopra, Wayne Dyer, Stuart Wilde and so many other awesome souls who have taught me so much! I wouldn't have done that if I hadn't picked up a publication that informed me about these great minds who were going to be touring in Australia many years ago. My intuition said, "Call the promoter, and you will be invited to sing on this tour!" If I had gone with the logistics of this happening, then I would have never made that call. However, I did make the call, and I did go on that tour...and I sang and sang and sang! I got to meet these wonderful minds and hang out with them. They are the most amazing, wonderful people! However, it also made me realize that they are just people...like you and me... people who woke up! We can all wake up instead of slowly sleepwalking ourselves safely to death. I do not listen to anyone who says, "Oh, don't try that; you can't do it." It is the reason why I rarely ask for peoples' opinions anymore. I simply listen to the Infinite who tells me what to do. This is who I am. I am that I am! The voice about which I talk is really my very own spirit, one that is connected and One with the Infinite.

Wilma: That is so true! When I need to make a decision now, rather than asking another's opinion, I'll meditate onit. Sometimes I have to meditate on it for several days before the answer really becomes clear. I know that since I've been meditating, I have had so many wonderful experiences!

Okay....Let's now Be Still and Listen and BREATHE!....

Intuition

I now breathe in all of the good there is from The Infinite Mind. I am now One with The Infinite. Just as instinct guides the animals of our beautiful planet, I now allow and open myself to The Infinite Omniscience and allow this Divine Mind to operate through me.

I simply know without any required process of reasoning. God knows only intuitively and I know through this Divine Intuition.
Thank you God for always guiding me to my highest good. I hear Your voice with the gentleness of a breeze, flowing to and through me with ease and grace.

I love myself and I love you God! I thank you for all of my gifts and I know that from this moment onward, that all is well. I let go and I let You guide me, oh Dearest One. You are closer that my own breath and I am always here,
waiting to be the vehicle for Your Divine Plan for me.
Thy Will Be Done.

... And so it is.

Notes

Hi again from Wilma and Michele!

Thank you for reading our book. We enjoyed putting this together for you! It has helped us reinforce our thirst for spiritual unity through our growing and learning. This was a joy-filled project! We have learned that, in order to continue our spiritual awareness, we must constantly reinforce our spiritual education. Otherwise, it is so easy to slip into the collective thought.

We suggest, in order to gain the most benefit from this book, use our affirmations daily. Put them up where you can see them all the time...mirrors, refrigerators, cars, clocks... anywhere you will constantly be reminded... to help you grow in true love and understanding.

We wish you blessings, love and multi-dimensional abundance!

Love and Blessings,

Wilma and Michele

P.S. To contact Michele Blood via e-mail, please write to MusiVation@aol.com.
    To contact Michele via Web, write to www.MusiVation.com. Also, please call for your free MusiVation™ catalog at (800) 547-5601.

To contact Wilma McIntyre via e-mail, please write to wilma@wilmamcintyre.com.
Web: www.wilmamcintyre.com. Or call her at (800) 905-7923.

MICHELE'S MUSIVATION™
INTERNATIONAL, LLC

P.O. BOX 12933 • LA JOLLA, CA 92039-2933
PHONE: (800) 547-5601 FAX: (858) 459-3032
E-MAIL: MusiVation@aol.com WEBSITE: www.MusiVation.com

Order 20 or more products in any combination, and received a 20% discount
Order 50 or more products in any combination, and received an exciting 40% discount!
This Order Form is 2 pages

MusiVation™ Product	US$ Price	Quantity	Total
Create Miracles and Heal Your Life	$19.95 ISBN 1-890679-09-7		
Michele's Magnetic Creative Visualization	$19.95 ISBN 1-890679-19-4		
Michele's Goal Setting and Affirmation Power Audio Program	$12.95 ISBN 1-890679-22-4		
It's Your Tonight - Pop song CD by Michele & Quino	$6.95		
Affirmation Power with Michele 6 Cassette Program	$69.95 ISBN 1-890679-20-8		
SONGS for SUCCESS by Michele -CD	$14.95 ISBN 1-890679-08-9		
SONGS for SUCCESS by Michele - Cassette	$10.95 ISBN 1-890679-23-2		
New Paradigms with Bob Proctor and Michele 6-Cassette Program	$69.95 1-890679-06-2		
Be a Magnet to Money Audio Program with Bob Proctor and Michele Blood	$19.95 ISBN 1-890679-03-8		
Be Your Perfect Weight Audio Program with Bob Proctor and Michele	$19.95 ISBN 1-890679-00-3		
How To Get Happy, Stay Happy And Live Happily Ever After Audio Program by Chris Michaels	$12.95 ISBN 1-890679-01-1		
Finding True Love by Asara Lovejoy and Michele Blood	$19.95 ISBN 1-890679-15-1		
Choices For Success by D. Michael Rideout and Michele Blood	$12.95 ISBN 1-890679-18-6		
Conversations on Money, Sex and Spirituality Book with Wilma and Michele	$14.95 ISBN#1-890679-17-8		

Subtotal:	$
Sales Tax: California addresses add 7.25% of total	$
Shipping and Handling: add $3.95 for the first item and $1.00 for each additional item to the same address	$
Less 20% discount for 20-49 products ordered	
Less 40% discount for 50 or more products ordered	$
Outside U.S. and Canada: call or e-mail for postage rates.	
Total:	**$**

Name: .... Order Date:_____..........

Street:...

City... State..................... Zip.................. Country........................

Phone: ....Fax:...

E-Mail: ....Website:...

( ) Check ( ) Visa ( ) Mastercard ( ) American Express

Credit card number...Expiration date ....

How did you hear about us?..

....

Notes

Notes

Notes

Notes

Notes

Notes

Notes

Notes

Notes

Notes